LIGHTERS

Collectible
LIGHTERS

Juan Manuel Clark

Flammarion

Series editor: Frédérique Crestin-Billet
Translated from the French by Jonathan Sly
Copy-edited by Penelope Isaac
Proofreader: Christine Schultz-Touge
Design by Lélie Carnot
Typesetting by Thierry Renard
Originally published as La Folie des Briquets
© 2002 Flammarion, Paris
English-language edition © Flammarion, Inc.

ISBN : 2-0801-1133-7
Printed in France

In my mind, the Ford Fairlane 500, Kentucky bourbon, Salem menthol cigarettes, and Zippo cigarette lighters all roll into one—the same dream, of America and freedom. And all thanks to you, G.I. Dan. You were stationed just outside Paris, France, at the start of the 1960s. You were introducing us to those small wonders of U.S. industry, and our parents' Renault 4s, liters of red wine, Gauloises cigarettes with their blue logo, and matchboxes all paled in comparison. By the end of the day, we had all been for a good spin in the Fairlane. We had smoked all your Salems and the bottle of Bourbon was empty. But you left your Zippo lighter with me—along with a huge thirst for the United States of America. I still have them today.

CONTENTS

Introduction

Cigarette lighters, as we know them today, are very recent inventions. It is difficult to imagine that, less than a hundred years ago, such a basic article did not exist. Since my grandfathers' youth—not so long ago; but in the space of three small generations—the way we make fire has undergone three major evolutions, or revolutions. More than it has in over a million years!

It has been an age or two since man first started harnessing fire—about 700,000 years ago, if the experts are to be believed. When lightning or excessive drought made fire appear spontaneously, man would thank the gods and would foster it carefully. Man had probably already observed the sparks emitted when two flint stones collided, as his tools, arrowheads, and the knives that he spent long hours making were all based on this mineral. Maybe it was as he was making tools that a spark landed on dry leaves and he made his discovery—or that they made their discoveries. Because it is highly unlikely that one man in isolation was the sole discoverer of fire. Perhaps in the same era, at several points around the globe, other human beings were also identifying this vital phenomenon.

The other firelighting technique discovered by men in early times was to rub together two pieces of dry wood until they

The rubbing method of making fire has survived over thousands of years and is still practiced by remote populations.

were burning sufficiently to start a fire. There is a real art to this method of making fire. In her book *Ishi in Two Worlds* (University of California Press, 1988), Theodora Kroeber relates how, in 1911, her husband adopted Ishi, a native American Indian and last remaining member of the "wild" Yahi tribe. The work recorded Ishi's actions as he went about his daily chores, in particular the way he and his tribesmen made fire, as they had done for thousands of years. "Before he starts actually rubbing, Ishi spreads dry moss, thistledown, or the shredded lining of willow bark in the notch and along the groove [of a section of softwood, called the "fireboard," Ed.], as well as on the ground beneath the groove. Then he crouches, holding each end of the fireboard down against the ground with his toes. Placing the wide end of the drill in the notch, and taking it between his hands, palms open, pressed against each other, he twists the drill to and fro. His hands also

The tale of Ishi's adventures is a poignant account of Native American life, customs, and techniques.

Théodora Kroeber

Ishi

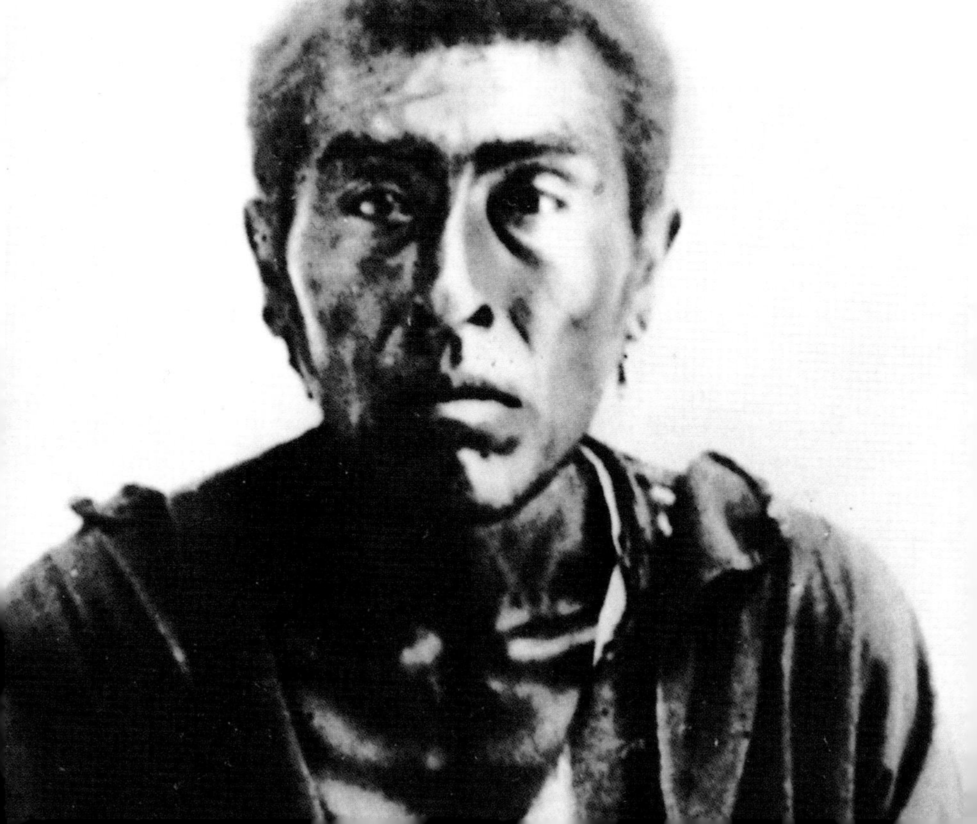

press downward, applying pressure, in such a way that the drill's turbine movement grinds into the bottom of the cavity, producing a fine sawdust at the edges that starts to brown and smoke occasionally, then to char, and finally to produce definite smoke." This same way of making fire was noted by the anthropologist Doctor Maes in the Belgian Congo during the 1930s. He describes it in his work dated August 1933, entitled *Les Allume-Feu du Congo belge* ("Firelighters of the Belgian Congo"), published in the annals of the Belgian Congo Museum in Tervueren, Belgium.

In the eighth century B.C.E., iron metallurgy

Flint, a tinder cord, and a steel plate decorated with an insect was typical of the equipment used to make fire up to the middle of the nineteenth century

became more widespread, and mankind went one better than hitting flint against flint. Now flint was struck against iron. When this happens, particles of molten metal fly off—the sparks. Iron meant progress. The next great advance was the arrival of steel, in the twelfth century. Its iron-carbon mixture provides larger, brighter, hotter sparks, and more of them. Steel had to be imported into France from Germany, Damas, and Sweden. It was not until 1722 that the French physicist René Réamur started producing steel on an industrial scale in France. During the process of experimentation, iron pyrites, iron's natural sulphite, with its gold-hued crystals, replaced flint for striking.

In China, lighters of this type are still used to strike flint.

INTRODUCTION

For hundreds of thousands of years, men and women had roamed around carrying with them a small leather bag containing their valuable firemaking tools. The bag contained dry moss, small sticks of tinder, and sections of wood suitable for fire-starting, including the red-flowered chestnut tree (Ishi's preferred wood). Later, with the development of arts and crafts, the leather bag became the tinderbox, and was decorated with various natural objects—shells, whale or crocodile teeth, nuts, or elephant ivory. From the end of the fifteenth century onward, an important invention made its own contribution to our need to make fire: the flintlock pistol. This device functions on the same principle as the cigarette lighter, striking flint against steel. Later, in the seventeenth century, the harquebus—a heavy matchlock gun usually fired from a support—represented an important development, and the first tabletop firelighters were constructed on this principle, using the firing system of weaponry. Such articles were not in wide circulation: they were the reserve of the elite. The pistol-shaped flint firelighter continued to be manufactured until the end of the nineteenth century.

Pistol and lighter interacted in the seventeenth century.
Their firing methods are identical.

Fire-kindling was still necessary, however, and it had a long and bright future ahead. The refinement of the Renaissance and Enlightenment brought an esthetic dimension to the creation of practical firelighters, with the finest craftsmen producing beautiful designs. Early advances in physics and chemistry in the eighteenth century moved the harnessing of fire on a step, but not greatly. Wheel-lock and rack

An eighteenth century gentleman would have used this lighter to create sparks to light his pipe. Note also the presence of a barrel cleaner, bullet puller, pipe tamper, and pipe cleaner.

Lighters

The category of lighter might also include some of mankind's other attempts to tame fire. In Antiquity, we tried to harness the rays of the sun by magnifying them to create flames. The idea was revived in the eighteenth century, though with little success, as fire can only be made this way on sunny days. A fire piston is another ancient process, used mainly in Asia, as bamboo is very effective in its construction. It works on the principle that compressed gases heat up and, with the use of a piston resembling a miniature bicycle pump, it is possible to set tinder alight by compressing the air around it. It is also known as an "adiabatic" fire-starter: the butane is compressed without heat being extracted, resulting in a rise in the gas's temperature.

systems for firelighting appeared, but these were simply mechanical ways of striking flint against steel. They were bulky, expensive, and the preserve of the rich, those people who actually needed them the least. The man on the street still had to hammer flint against iron.

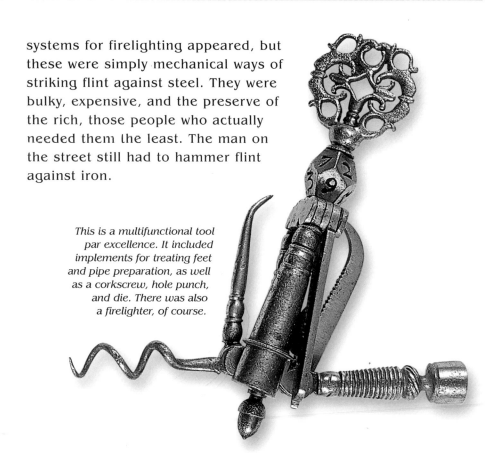

This is a multifunctional tool par excellence. It included implements for treating feet and pipe preparation, as well as a corkscrew, hole punch, and die. There was also a firelighter, of course.

Beautiful firelighters were crafted by artisans of the era. There were simple, sober appliances as well as marvelous multifunctional tools, (the Lesecq des Tournelles museum in Rouen, France, has a fine collection). These ingenious contraptions might have included, besides the firelighter, a corkscrew, screwdriver, and tamper for pipes, pincers for picking embers from the hearth, a hoof pick, a punch to make holes in a leather bridle, a penknife to sharpen goose feathers for quills, or a die to decide who was going to pick up the check in the tavern.

It is said that if smoking was banned in churches, it was because of the disturbance caused by the noise of lighters constantly being struck to light pipes. Obviously, preaching becomes troublesome in such conditions.

Matches have been widely used in homes for a long time, but they were different from those we use today. They were simply thin strips of paper or small pieces of trimmed wood used to transit fire from a constantly burning hearth, perhaps to a pipe, or to a pile of leaves heaped in the courtyard of a farm. In cstaminets, small cafés, when customers asked for a light, they would receive a small pot containing a burning ember. Pipes were available from a rack for the use of any customer, as long as they returned them before leaving. The forerunner of today's matchstick came in the form of books

It took a considerable amount of academic effort and chemical experimentation to arrive at the safety match.

soaked in melted sulfur that would only burn if placed in a naked flame. The first chemically produced matches date from 1809. They were also soaked in sulfur, then dipped in a mixture that contained sulfur, potassium chlorate, club moss, and gum water. To light them, they had to be dipped in sulphuric acid. Not the simplest of methods.

Wall-hanging firelighters were much in fashion in public buildings at the end of the nineteenth and the start of the twentieth century. They came in diverse and surprising forms.

I n 1816, the French physicist Louis-Charles Derosne made a major breakthrough. With Baron Gagniard de Latour, he had the idea of heating particles of phosphorus in a flask then removing them using a matchstick. When cold, and if rubbed against a felt surface, the particles would burst into flame. The phosphorus would then light the sulfur which, in turn, would ignite the wood. Such materials react perfectly, except the reaction itself is extremely dangerous. Finally in 1831, the French chemist Charles Sauria came up with the idea of phosphorus-based matches, an invention claimed by Kammener; though, rather than discovering the process, he simply adapted it for production on an industrial scale. In 1833, Kammener opened the first match factory. But the product was responsible for a number of fires that flared up unexpectedly. Children were among the first victims. A German chemistry professor, Anton Schrotter, improved the process, but it was a Swede, Johan Edvard Lundstom,

Flint lighters have been designed in all shapes and sizes. The shape of the striking iron is fairly typical here.

who removed the phosphorus from the match and placed it on the side of the box. The two highly inflammable ingredients were thus kept separate. And kazaam! The safety match was born. During Napoleon's imperial reign in France (1796–1815), Lorentz invented a device that lit a jet of hydrogen with a spark. In 1823, the French physicist and chemist Joseph Louis Gay-Lussac invented the flameless lighter, which functioned with a platinum mesh. Finally, in 1860, French physicist Gaston Planté invented the ring lighter.

This electric lighter from the 1890s works like a wet battery, with three electrodes (in the reservoir on the side) that create the spark. The gasoline is stored in the large tank.

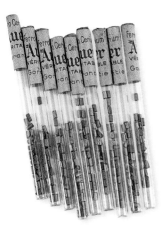

Firelighting made spectacular progress with the development of these tiny stones by the Austrian, Karl Auer.

With oil drilling in its pioneer days, Austrian chemist Karl Auer discovered ferrocerium. The conjunction of the two innovations soon generated the first friction ignition lighters, known as "striker lighters." The invention of lighter flints, sparked against a jagged wheel, gave the lighter the boost it needed. In France, it was the frontline soldiers of the First World War—known as the "poilus," or "hairy ones"—in their trenches, who gave the lighter back to the people. The French state was ever vigilant to this sudden interest, however. With the population clamoring to possess a lighter, their market increased and an indirect tax was soon enforced on anybody who used one—in other words, nearly all the male and half the female population. A country-dweller at the start of the twentieth century may not have had a French franc in his pocket, but he would have had a lighter, a handkerchief, and a knife—his essential equipment. The law

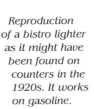

Reproduction of a bistro lighter as it might have been found on counters in the 1920s. It works on gasoline.

Between 1911 and 1945, the French state levied a tax on the lighter.

passed in France in 1910 forced lighter manufacturers to pay a tax on their product, however, one that was passed onto customers. Producers, from this point on, were subject to revokable authorization from the tax authorities. In the words of the law: "The only lighters exempt from the tax are those composed of a flint, a steel shaft, and a wick of touchwood." Some relief.

F rom then on lighters were checked and stamped to prove that the tax office had indeed received its dues. The first stamp used, in 1911, featured both date and year. Consequently, stamps became uniform, adopting two different standardized formats depending on the size of the lighter. The strip of metal bearing the stamp may seem charming today, but it was deemed unsightly at the time; indeed, top-of-the-range-models in France were instead discreetly stamped with the letters BL ("*briquet de luxe*") to indicate that they were "luxury lighters." War was looming and soldiers left for the front bedecked with flowers, promising to return before Christmas. The month was August; the year was 1914.

Antoine Rivarol (1753–1801) declared that "man is the only animal to make fire—it is this that gives him his dominion over the world." On the left is a gasoline and tinder lighter.

The foot-soldiers, the poilus, in the trenches at the front went crazy about this new way of making fire. The lighter was so easy to use, so simple to make: it became their emblem. They cobbled together thousands of them, in their barracks, in the trenches, even far behind the lines. They even set up workshops to make extra money. Production of the most elementary articles only took a few hours. Manufacturing lighters, like making weapons when there are not enough to go around, was all about being resourceful—recycling, modifying, and immediate application. Obviously, soldiers at the front did not pay tax on their lighters. It is hard to imagine a tax inspector, dressed in starched collar and spectacles, turning up on the doorstep of an ex-poilu and demanding to know if the household lighter, made from a German belt-buckle, is covered under the tax law of December 28, 1910. Patrice Wavrin's work on lighters in the First World War, entitled *Craftwork of the Trenches and Poilu Lighters*, describes this episode of tax office opportunism perfectly. The tax was set at two francs per metal pocket lighter and five francs per silver lighter. The tax rose to twenty francs if the lighter was made of gold or platinum. For table or desk lighters, in other words any lighter more than four inches (ten centimeters) high, the tax rose to five francs for metal ones, ten francs for silver, and fifty francs for gold or platinum. In some cases, particularly on cheaper models, the tax effectively doubled the retail price.

In addition there were laws in place to prohibit lighter manufacture, even for personal use. The crackdown on offenders centered (fortunately) on unpatented products and forgeries, which were tax-stamped illicitly and sold for a quarter of the price.

In a matter of months, poilus at the war front turned the lighter from a luxury product to an item of mass consumption.

Despite taxation, sales of gasoline lighters of all shapes and sizes soared on postwar markets. The next chapter in the history of cigarette lighters was automatization. From the 1920s onwards, to ignite a lighter (top-of-the-range ones, at least), one no longer had to open it then flick the wheel. All that was needed was to press a button that lifted the cap and exposed the wick, while simultaneously sparking the flint via a spring mechanism. The only drawback was if the button was accidentally pressed in a pocket.... Many a handbag or pair of pants suffered as a result.

An ad from the 1930s for Lancel lighters,
all of which are inspired by the perennially
fashionable Dunhill lighter.

Un seul briquet pratique
L'automatique "Lancel"
Tramere

G. L. Manuel Frères

N- 1
300 fr.

N- 2
160 fr.

Then came the butane lighter, the brainchild of Marcel Quercia, a Frenchman, working with his assistant Georges Ferdinand. This innovation was manufactured and marketed by Flaminaire and revolutionized the lighting of cigarettes, as well as home fires and bonfires. It enabled the creation of beautiful lighters that no longer smelled of gasoline, that did not leak, and that did not mar the flavor of tobacco. To replenish an empty lighter, smokers now only had to return to the tobacconist to exchange their standard butane cartridge. The cartridge was returned to the factory for a refill, while the fresh one was being used. This golden age for the refuel-able lighter only lasted until the end of the 1960s. The era of the disposable lighter had arrived—along with that of the disposable razor, disposable ballpoint, and much more. Strange times indeed!

The lighter entered a new age in terms of reliability and technique with butane. But life for the gasoline-fueled Zippo (right) was not over quite yet.

I

WORKADAY
lighters

The lighters in this chapter were of little value when they were made, but they were nevertheless reliable and durable. Being able to produce fire on demand is no mean feat, even if the materials involved are crude and their design rudimentary. Whether Japanese, French, or German, they are much sought after by collectors, who appreciate the forgotten techniques they represent.

*Flint and
tinder-wick
lighters came in
all shapes and sizes.
They consisted of a rigid
support to grip, and a hole for
the wick onto which the sparks
could be projected. A cap, connected
to a chain, was fixed to one end
of the wick, enabling it to be snuffed out.*

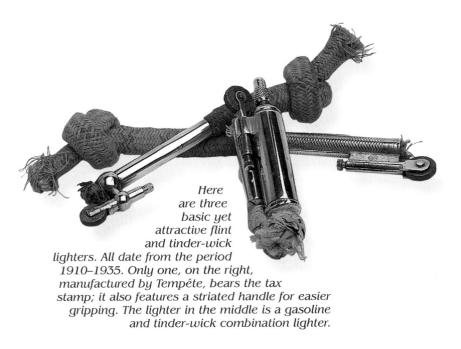

Here
are three
basic yet
attractive flint
and tinder-wick
lighters. All date from the period
1910–1935. Only one, on the right,
manufactured by Tempête, bears the tax
stamp; it also features a striated handle for easier
gripping. The lighter in the middle is a gasoline
and tinder-wick combination lighter.

This flint and tinder-wick lighter does not have a wheel mechanism to create sparks but, instead, a shaft with a steel tip that is rubbed back and forth on the upper part of the solid silver box. The end of the tinder wick is thus in contact with the sparks that are produced. The box is nearly 1¾ inches (4.2 cm) long.

*In the 1920s, just such a low-cost flint
and tinder-wick lighter was common
in rural communities.
This one is marked Bono Jem, Paris.*

An example of a primer lighter using mercury fulminate, which would crackle and light the wick above the gasoline chamber (on the left, inside). This particular model is French, but they were also manufactured in the United States and Germany.

This curious-shaped cigarette case is also a lighter. Probably of British origin, it is marked with the BooM brand name; its patent number 13093/10. We know by the tax mark that it was sold in France. The wick of this gasoline lighter lit by flicking the knob on the left, after the square metal cover protecting it had been lifted. It is 3½ inches (9 cm) long.

*This is a fairly worn,
semi-automatic lighter
in chrome-plated brass.
The small lever,
top left, uncovers
the wick before
the wheel is
flicked to create
the necessary
sparks.*

A gasoline and tinder-wick combination lighter. The gasoline was introduced from below and the wick appeared by unscrewing the cap above. If the gasoline ran out, the head could pivot so that it was adjacent to the tinder wick. No doubt a product of the trenches. It is 3½ inches (9 cm) high.

At the end of the 1940s, when the first jet aircraft started breaking speed records, this flameless lighter appeared. Dubbed "the jet lighter," it was patented "SGDG"— without government guarantee. Simply unscrew the wheel at the top to introduce the air necessary to light the cigarette, the tip of which was placed in the hole at the top of the lighter.

Bearing an uncanny resemblance to lipstick cases, these flameless lighters were targeted at American women. They were made by Vestalux and their license number was 1.946.719. This shape was frequently copied for a host of other lighters.

The case is on the left
and the cap is on the right.
This American pocket lighter
has a catalytic ignition,
and was manufactured
by Master-Lite around 1928.
Note the metal frame protruding
from the cap on the right
that protected the filaments,
as well as the small platinum
ball that catalyzes the reaction
when it is dropped into the
center of the wider cylinder.

This flameless lighter is French.
It is a "self allumeur," meaning
"self-lighting." It was made
in Paris and issued with
a government patent.
Once opened, it separated
into two cylinders of different
diameter. Methanol, in contact
with a platinum mesh, causes
a chemical reaction, producing
enough heat to light a cigarette.
The first drag on the cigarette
was maybe not such a treat!

This American lighter made by Vestalux is made of aluminum and functions using a catalytic reaction involving ethanol, methanol, or any other rectified alcohol. Another American brand, Jifty-Lite, made in Titusville, Florida, worked on the same principle.

This table lighter is marked "Polaire 75-8, made in France." The brand is Polaire and the name of the model is "Le Brésilien." To light the cigarette, the shaft should be lifted to release the wick, before flicking the wheel. It is 2½ inches (6.5 cm) high.

Battery-powered table lighter with filament. The battery also powers the small bulb on the top right of the lighter, making this accessory multifunctional. Manufactured by Fumalux in 1963.

Hexagonal nickel-plated table lighter. It is gasoline fueled. Note the tax mark beneath the ignition mechanism, a reminder of the lighter tax existing in France between 1911 and 1945.

Like the model
on the facing page,
this is a table lighter.
This one, however,
functions on butane gas.
It was manufactured
by Flaminaire around
1950 and was their
3½-inch (9-cm) high
"Baronet" model.

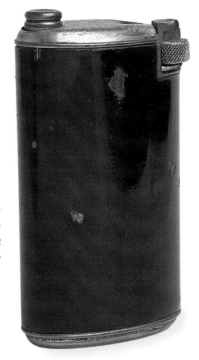

Every taste should be catered for and cigarette lighter manufacturers make the most of this rule. Butane lighter mechanisms, with their butane reservoirs, were factory-made...

...and adapted to any object, such as this block of resin with a geisha girl inside, this imitation oil lamp, and even a tank (page 192).

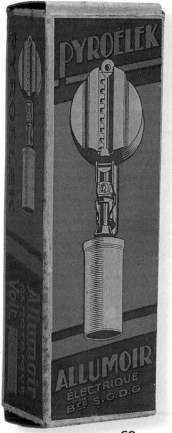

"If you are satisfied, recommend the Pyroélek to your friends!" Such is the request on the back of the box containing this electric lighter manufactured in the 1930s. It operated on 100–140 volts and was fitted to the wall of the kitchen.

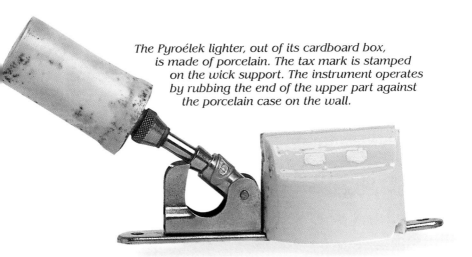

The Pyroélek lighter, out of its cardboard box, is made of porcelain. The tax mark is stamped on the wick support. The instrument operates by rubbing the end of the upper part against the porcelain case on the wall.

The gasoline here is stored in the nickel-plated reservoir. This wall-mounted lighter works by producing an electric spark between the wick, on the left, and an element situated inside. It is 2 inches (5 cm) wide and 4 inches (10 cm) high.

*The Crok-Flamm Pirouett of the 1930s
worked by igniting a gasoline-soaked wick
with an electric spark. The hole in the
middle provides a convenient way
of extinguishing the wick.*

The delightfully monikered "Le Cuistot" or "The Chef" was a wall-mounted lighter with a very specific purpose. The button top right freed a spring that ignited the wick over the gasoline cylinder, bottom right, which has here been removed from its base.

Often a lighter's tax mark is hidden away. This is not the case with this Bakelite wall lighter. The French state taxed items that were considered indispensable, such as bicycles and windows, as well as lighters. This lighter has no brand name printed on it. There is an identical Dutch model of the same epoch, however, that was marketed as the "Electric Lucifer."

This very elegant flat lighter
dating from 1920 contains a
roll of tinder that is pushed
out using the notched
wheel on the left.
The spark wheel in
the center ignites
the tinder while
the box is closed.
The smoker simply
opens the cover
and places the tip
of his cigarette over
the gentle flame.

This slender lighter is more sophisticated in appearance and was designed to be slipped into women's handbags. It carries no brand name, but was produced about 1930.

Both of these intriguing lighters have been made from recycled Michelin tire valves. The one on the left has a protective wick cap made from a bicycle valve cap, courtesy again of Michelin. The one on the right has a removable lid connected to a short chain, making it easy to slip into a pocket without further wear on lining materials.

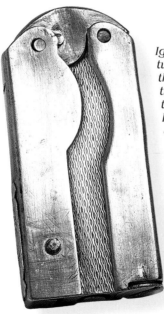

Igniting a lighter using just two fingers is easier than flipping a lid, flicking the wheel, then shaking to extinguish the flame before replacing the cap, even when the last two steps are rolled into one. Patented lighter by Kaba.

This steel lighter, of slightly clumsy design, was made by an amateur, based on a patented model and using a recycled case. It is unlikely it was made by a poilu since, in 1914, these frontline soldiers had large amounts of brass and copper at their disposal, so they tended not to use steel.

This French lighter works by pulling
the two ends of the tube to produce a spark.
The traditional wheel has been replaced
by a straight striated rod. The gasoline is poured
in on the left by unscrewing the cap.
Note the mark attesting to payment
of the lighter tax, instituted by the law
of December 28, 1910.

This item may resemble a pocket watch, but is in fact a gasoline lighter. It is 1¾ inches high (4.8 cm), made of chrome-plated brass with a geometric pattern, and is a Swiss model, patented in 1934.

This lighter was offered as a gift to the prolific collector, Alain Berthon, who admits that it is not the most attractive of his collection. It is a fairly standard version of a German watch-lighter. The erect vertical section is the wick cover.

Lighter manufactured by Browers, in Kalamazoo, Michigan. The city itself has been home to a great many manufacturing industries producing objects such as fishing reels, fountain pens, and timepieces. This is a simple gasoline model with a hinged wick cover, 2¾ inches (7 cm) high.

*A variation on the book-shaped
gasoline lighter, this was no doubt
made by a soldier in the trenches.
It is 3¼ inches (8 cm) long.*

Lighters can be used
to convey symbols
and constitute a sign
of belonging to a
group. Here and
on the facing page
are two lighters
that carry symbols
of the Freemasons.

The Freemason's lighter on the facing page was made by SGFVB in Paris and measures 2¾ inches (7.2 cm). This one measures 2½ inches (6.8 cm). Both bear the French tax mark, indicating that they were in use between 1911 and 1945.

*This small silver pocket lighter
measures 1¾ inches (4.4 cm) high
and is marked "Myon 201."*

The small ring on the left enables the gasoline reservoir to be opened so that the pocket lighter can be filled. The lighter may also be attached to a belt or button using this ring. It is ignited by pressing the button on the top right and was produced in the 1930s by Thorens, a Swiss manufacturer.

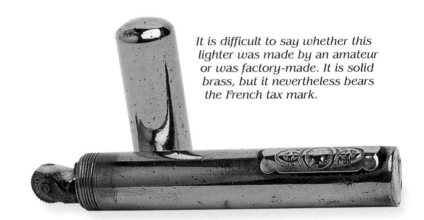

It is difficult to say whether this lighter was made by an amateur or was factory-made. It is solid brass, but it nevertheless bears the French tax mark.

Made from nickel-plated brass, the "Le Pratique" table gasoline lighter features a SGDG patent, which means it is patented without quality guarantee from the French government. The cylinder is also marked with a five-pronged star. Note the trace of the government tax mark that has been removed. The gasoline is introduced in the lighter via the base, which unscrews.

Risqué images have always been very popular as designs for tobacco accessories in general. Pouches, files, pipes, and snuffboxes have been emblazoned with nymphets of all shapes and sizes, and in the scantiest of attires.

Here and facing page, the two sides of the same French lighter, dating back to the 1920s. Although manufactured industrially, it does not feature the government tax mark.

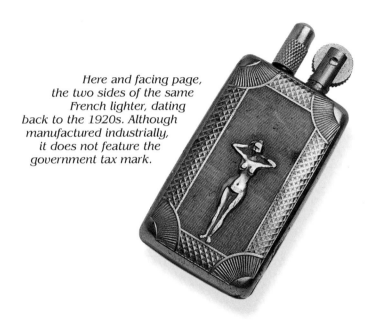

The simplest and cheapest lighter of all is no doubt this small cylinder, which could easily be confused with a tube of lipstick at the bottom of a bag. It is 1¾ inches (4.5 cm) high and was made in aluminum by Polaire in Paris around 1950.

Press this lighter down and the flame will appear at one of the windows. Made of aluminum, it is 2¾ inches (7.1 cm) high, and marked "Cop Patent, Paris."

An automatic lighter is one where a simple flick of a switch suffices to set in motion the mechanisms necessary to ignite the wick. Here the button is on the right of the image above the French government tax mark on the side. 2½ inches (6.2 cm) high.

This model was designed for sheltering cigarettes and pipes from a draft when lighting them. The wick should be uncovered before flicking the spark wheel downward. Made by the French brand Le Touriste, it is 2½ inches (6.2 cm) high.

Despite its name, the "Winchester," this lighter was made in France. It is made of nickel-plated chrome, is gasoline fueled and is 2¼ inches (5.7 cm) high. By pressing in the left side, the cap lifts, activating the spark wheel, so the lighter ignites.

These low-cost table lighters came in dozens of models. They were all the rage in France in the 1930s and would be found placed with pride on coffee tables in the humblest of dwellings. This one with its wraparound glossy picture has a certain charm.

*Small, easily portable lighters were very popular
before disposable lighters became the standard for
smokers. On the left is a Japanese Prince brand
lighter. The one on the right has no brand.
Each measures ¾ inch (2.1 cm) high.*

*This Swiss Rodan Lighter is decorated with
an alpine mountain scene on one side and
a map of Switzerland on the other.
The cylindrical and domino-shaped lighters
are unbranded.*

This imposing table lighter is nearly 4 inches (10 cm) high. When opened, it is obvious that its mechanism is no different from that of a pocket lighter. However, it has the extra feature of a hidden brush to clean the wick, as well as a supply of flints.

The Chinese were the first to mass-produce low-cost gasoline lighters and export them worldwide. This is a Sunflower lighter, featuring a country scene on one side and a more industrial view on the other.

The switch on the right needs to be spun vigorously to generate the sparks required to light a cigarette. The tip of the cigarette is slipped into the hole on the top of the lighter. There is no naked flame with this model, as the tobacco lights on contact with the sparks produced. It is made by Transfo, in aluminum, patented to W. D'Alton in 1948.

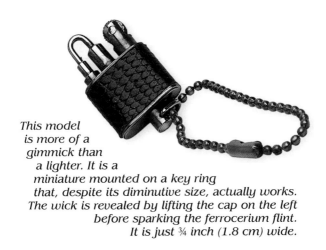

This model
is more of a
gimmick than
a lighter. It is a
miniature mounted on a key ring
that, despite its diminutive size, actually works.
The wick is revealed by lifting the cap on the left
before sparking the ferrocerium flint.
It is just ¾ inch (1.8 cm) wide.

This lighter displays the emblem of the Mediterranean island of Corsica; other French provinces would have had their own model. The box has exactly the same dimensions as a packet of the French cigarettes, Gauloises, and would have stopped their soft packet from being crushed in a pocket or handbag. On top is the simple cylindrical lighter that functions on gasoline. It was manufactured by Util in Paris.

This lighter features the name of a French rugby team, Luz Olympique, represented by the tool of their trade. It is made of boxwood and contains a lighter that was sold in the 1950s by the team. 2½ inches (6.2 cm) high.

Lighter designers have thought
of everything, including this surprising orange-plastic
match dispenser. It may be considered as a lighter,
since the match, released using the knob above,
lights by friction and remains held in place while
it is alight. This model was made in Clermont-Ferrand
in central France in the 1970s.

The Flamidor
"Flambeau" or "torch"
is a gasoline lighter
designed for pipe
smokers. Its flame is
protected from drafts
in the cylindrical
recess, which is then
closed by pressing
the milled plug above.
The 3½ cubic inch
(9 cm³) gasoline
reservoir can be
refilled via the base.

This ingenious model featuring the logo of the French police appeared on the market at a bad time, just as gasoline lighters were becoming history. The button on the left activates a small pump that moistens the wick on demand before the spark wheel is flicked. In this way the gasoline stays in a sealed reservoir, which limits its evaporation considerably.

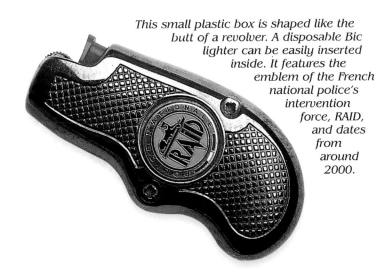

This small plastic box is shaped like the butt of a revolver. A disposable Bic lighter can be easily inserted inside. It features the emblem of the French national police's intervention force, RAID, and dates from around 2000.

If there is one lighter that holds a special place in the popular imagination, it is the Zippo. In France alone, 120,000 Zippos are sold each month. In the Zippo catalogue this one is labeled "Model # 200 Regular"...

...and has a "brush finished" case.
It is decorated with the portrait and
signature of "the king," Elvis Presley.
The lighter below is a "Slim # 1610"
model from June 1987. It has a "high
polished chrome"
finish.

The Zippo "Sport" collection was started in 1959; as well as this bowler, it featured a golfer, skiers, hunters, and fishermen. This lighter dates back to 1965.

The Zippo series has always been highly successful, and the aim of the game for collectors is to possess them all. The presidents of the great nations have been among those immortalized by Zippo. On the left is George Bush Senior with Mikhail Gorbachev, and on the right is Ronald Reagan, also in the company of the former president of the Soviet Union. The first dates from 1990 and the second from 1989.

As well as its factory in Bradford, Pennsylvania, Zippo also set up in Canada in the 1950s at Niagara Falls in Ontario. The factory produced this lighter displaying Quebec's flag in 1989. It is in its original plastic box.

This lighter, commemorating the 1980 Olympic Games, was actually produced in August 1990, ten years after the event, as part of a series on the Games. This particular lighter has never been opened, and still carries the sticker on the back connecting the case to the cap, which remains unbroken.

II

SOLDIERS'
lighters

Foot-soldiers in the First World War trenches, the French poilus, manufactured their own lighters. For the poilu, knee-deep in mud, and frostbitten through the chill winter, fire was life. The following pages show the ingenuity, talent, and innate sense of beauty that drove homesick soldiers to manufacture and decorate their own symbols of a lost life. The lighter industry naturally caught on quickly, and poilu lighters soon provided designs for versions behind the lines.

These pieces of popular art, like Zippo lighters from the Vietnam War (1965–73) after them, convey a uniquely emotional record of these historical events.

A true piece of popular art, this poilu lighter, painstakingly designed with a steel tip, is made of two convex shells welded together with tin. The snuff cap is a bicycle inner tube valve. The cap containing the flint, or ferrocerium, is a trade accessory.

The dedication on the shell of the lighter opposite reads "Greetings from your son." This lighter was obviously made for a soldier's beloved parents. Given its 2¾-inch (7-cm) width, it was probably designed for table or household use.

A copper coin was used to adorn
the sides of this lighter.
It was carefully filed
down to dispense with
its original face to leave
a surface ready for a
fresh engraving—A.R.,
the initials of its owner.
The markings "Verdun"
and "1916" on the back
attest to its origin.
On the other side
is an engraved
flower motif.

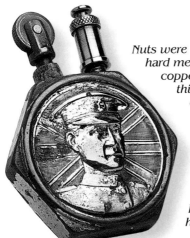

Nuts were usually fashioned from hard metal such as steel and copper and, despite its shape, this lighter is actually made of pewter. This would suggest that this "poilu-made" article was in fact industrially manufactured to imitate a recycled cannon or truck part. The steel-nut look has been enhanced by nickel plating, which has worn away over time.

Against the background
of the star-spangled
banner, this 1¾-inch
(4.2-cm) wide lighter
is decorated with
an American soldier,
wearing the U.S.
army's famous
regulation period
headwear. On the
other side is an
English "Tommy,"
or soldier, wearing
a cap, and set against
a Union Jack background.

This 3¼-inch (8.5-cm) wide lighter is a little broad to fit in a pocket. It was doubtless a table lighter, as it has a flat base enabling it to stand upright. It is made in zinc and so has a matte finish, which is enhanced on both sides by a flower of red copper. The gasoline is poured in by removing the cap bearing the spark wheel, flint, and spring.

This lighter, inscribed with
an allegory featuring
a British soldier, rifle
in hand, facing
the enemy, is
accompanied by
the fitting, if badly
spelled, slogan:
"Victorius Tommies."
Note the belt ring
to prevent losing
the lighter in combat.

Poilu lighters came in many different forms. Helmet or cap shapes (in this case from the British army) were often reproduced. This red copper and brass lighter is 1¾ inches (4.5 cm) in diameter. The wick and spark wheel are behind the visor.

It was easy to make this type of lighter using weapon cartridges. The base was machined so that it could be unscrewed and filled with gasoline-soaked cotton. The flint, spark wheel, and spring mechanism simply had to be soldered at the right height so that the sparks hit the wick directly. The screw thread around the wick suggests the snuff cap is missing. It stands 2¾ inches (7 cm) high.

This lighter is 2½ inches (6.6 cm) high, not including valves.

The left valve is from a bicycle, while the right one is from a motorcycle. There is no spark wheel or lighter flint, but a rod that sits permanently in the gasoline. The rod is attached to a wick and a small metal appendage that rubs against the bottom of the ferrocerium-coated lighter, providing a form of "striker lighter."

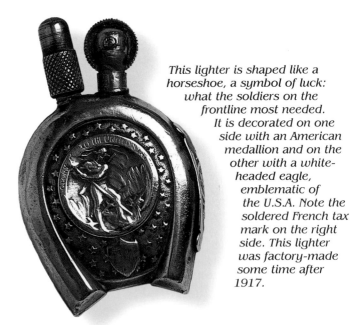

This lighter is shaped like a horseshoe, a symbol of luck: what the soldiers on the frontline most needed. It is decorated on one side with an American medallion and on the other with a white-headed eagle, emblematic of the U.S.A. Note the soldered French tax mark on the right side. This lighter was factory-made some time after 1917.

Manufactured from the buckle of a German army-issue belt. The wick-protection cap of this lighter, a bicycle inner tube valve, has been lost. The motto "Gott mit uns" means "God is with us" ("us" being the German army). Warmongers have always been eager to enlist God's help.

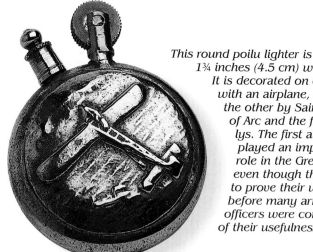

This round poilu lighter is 1¾ inches (4.5 cm) wide. It is decorated on one side with an airplane, and on the other by Saint Joan of Arc and the fleur-de-lys. The first airplanes played an important role in the Great War, even though they had to prove their worth before many army officers were convinced of their usefulness.

This industrially manufactured lighter features the portrait of Edith Cavell (1865–1915), a heroine of the First World War. An Englishwoman, she worked as a nurse in occupied Belgium, but was charged by the Germans with helping Allied soldiers escape to neutral Holland. She was arrested, tried, and shot dead.

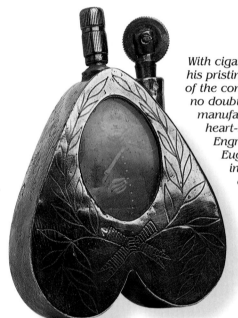

With cigarette in hand, wearing his pristine uniform at the start of the conflict, this soldier is no doubt responsible for the manufacture of this touching heart-shaped lighter. Engraved with the name Eugène Garde and the inscription "Souvenir of the 1914–1915 war," this lighter has taken its place in history.

This 1¾-inch (4.2-cm) wide
pocket lighter with a ring
was manufactured out of
a watch box or brass nut,
with its edges filed
or lathed. An allegory
inscribed with the
patriotic slogan "En
avant!" or "Forward!"
formed the basis of
this medallion, which was
on general sale in stores.

As long as the part is concave, anything— or almost anything— can make a lighter. Here, a door-handle of 2½ inches (6.1 cm) diameter is sealed to a circle of brass on the other side, which is decorated with an English penny coin, featuring Britannica, from 1918. Beside it is a smaller lighter, made from a German army-issue belt-buckle. On the bottom of the Iron Cross is the date—1914.

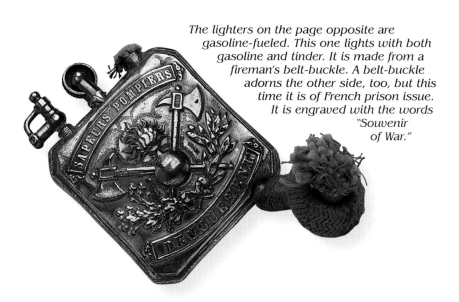

The lighters on the page opposite are gasoline-fueled. This one lights with both gasoline and tinder. It is made from a fireman's belt-buckle. A belt-buckle adorns the other side, too, but this time it is of French prison issue. It is engraved with the words "Souvenir of War."

Although it only measures 1¾ inches (4.8 cm) in diameter, this lighter is very heavy. It is made from a thick steel nut. On the side pictured there is a belt-buckle, and on the other a knight killing a dragon.

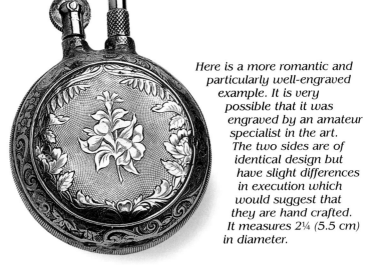

Here is a more romantic and particularly well-engraved example. It is very possible that it was engraved by an amateur specialist in the art. The two sides are of identical design but have slight differences in execution which would suggest that they are hand crafted. It measures 2¼ (5.5 cm) in diameter.

Despite the shape and materials used, this table lighter has probably not been made out of a shell case. Manufactured from a fine sheet of brass, it is a replica poilu lighter, many of which were factory-made during the 1920s. The missing cap in the photo is warhead-shaped.

This table lighter is made, on one side, from an English coin featuring King George V and a coin of the French Republic on the other. The main task for the coin's poilu manufacturer was to camber both sides to make them convex. Note that the cap protecting the wick is made with a rifle bullet.

The northern French towns of Lens, Roeux, and Bullecourt suffered considerably during the First World War. Here, their valiant defense is symbolized by a lion. This elegantly shaped lighter measures 2¼ inches (5.6 cm). The other side is made of brass and is not engraved.

This soldier's lighter is made of two coins. On the facing side is a picture of the heroic Albert I (1875–1934), the king of Belgium during the First World War, nicknamed the "Knight-King." On the other side is a Greek coin from 1930, proof that so-called "poilu lighters" were still being made well after the 1914–1918 war.

This nine-sided polygon was first fashioned before being soldered together. Coins from Arab countries were attached to each face before being expertly engraved by hand to create this exceptional and valuable item.

The inscription here reads "Foch—Generalissimo of the Allies," and accompanies a profile of the great man. This is a factory-produced lighter, on sale during and after the Great War. Ferdinand Foch (1851–1929) was appointed supreme generalissimo of the Allied armies on the Western front in April 1918.

Here and opposite are
the two sides of the
same novelty lighter.
It is made in the usual
style of a poilu lighter,
but was no doubt
factory-made. On this
side, a naked woman
admires herself
voluptuously...

...On the other, a soldier spies on her through the keyhole. The keyhole itself features on both sides of the lighter and is out of proportion. This lighter, with its fill screw at the bottom, was no doubt on sale after the First World War, but strangely carries no sign of the French tax mark. It is 1½ inches (4.2 cm) in diameter.

This is a variation on
the "erotic" scene of
the preceding pages.
This young lady is
wearing a little more
than her counterpart on
the other lighter, and
was perhaps designed
for the more prudish
soldier. However,
the soldier kneeling on
the other side of the door
(facing page) is identical
to the one on page 137.

The similarity of the two models suggests that this type of medallion or lighter design was sold in separate parts, including spark wheel and flint rod. All the poilu then had to do was to seal them together, in this case using a nut.

This lighter refuels on gasoline, inserted by unscrewing the base. The lighter is 4 inches (10 cm) high, and was made from a shell, then hand engraved. Note the red copper bands that helped the shell reach the necessary speeds.

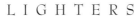

This model, also made from a shell, at 6¾ inches (17 cm) high, is much taller than its neighbor (facing page) and was clearly designed for table use. To light it, the small switch at the top, fitted with a multiplying mechanism, is flicked. The technical characteristics of shells— such as caliber, construction date and origin—are often indicated on the bottom of the cartridge.

Here and opposite are
two sides of the same
lighter. The cap, housing
the ferrocerium flint and
spark wheel, is missing.
This 1½-inch (3.6-cm)
wide model is factory-
made and is decorated
with the U.S. emblems
of the bald eagle and stars.

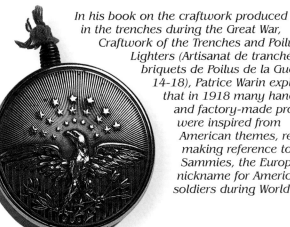

In his book on the craftwork produced
in the trenches during the Great War,
Craftwork of the Trenches and Poilu
Lighters (Artisanat de tranchée et
briquets de Poilus de la Guerre,
14-18), Patrice Warin explains
that in 1918 many hand-
and factory-made products
were inspired from
American themes, readily
making reference to
Sammies, the European
nickname for American
soldiers during World War I.

The poilu who made this lighter used a recycled watch box. Around the edges can be read, "European War 1914–1915;" the war's world dimension only came with the arrival of the Americans in 1917. On the other side are a biblical scene and the inscription Ave Maria Quis ut Deus Regina Angelorum Ora Pro N.

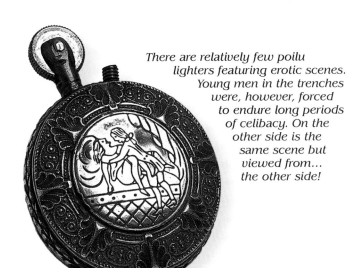

There are relatively few poilu
lighters featuring erotic scenes.
Young men in the trenches
were, however, forced
to endure long periods
of celibacy. On the
other side is the
same scene but
viewed from...
the other side!

This ¾-inch (2-cm) deep and 2¾-inch (7-cm) long lighter is intended for the table rather than the pocket. The mechanism has to pivot to be functional. The inscription "Amiens" on one side refers to the French town. On the other is an oak branch with leaves and acorns.

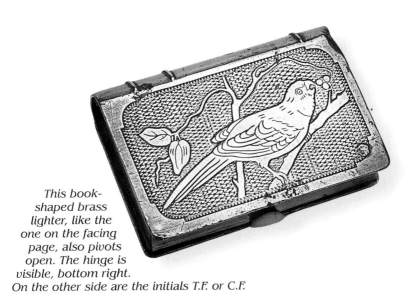

This book-shaped brass lighter, like the one on the facing page, also pivots open. The hinge is visible, bottom right. On the other side are the initials T.F. or C.F.

This is a more humble version
of the button lighters
on pages 152 to 153.
This button from
the Seventy-second
Heavy Artillery
division contains
the gasoline-soaked
cotton needed for the
reservoir. On the other
side, there is a simple
five-centimes coin
dated 1918.

This lighter required a certain technical know-how, which is why, even though it looks like a trench lighter, it is probably in fact factory-made. Furthermore, it is heavy; at such a weight its edges would soon make holes in a pocket. It is no doubt a table model, although its dimensions, 1¾ square inches (4.5 cm²), are modest.

The "Tiger" on this lighter is the French statesman Georges Clemenceau (1841–1929), the highly popular prime minister from November 1917, whose efforts were key to Allied success. Such homage is the least a poilu could pay him. On the reverse side is a portrait of General Foch, accompanied by the caption "Generalissimo of the Armies."

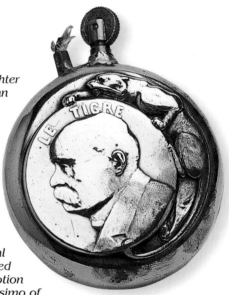

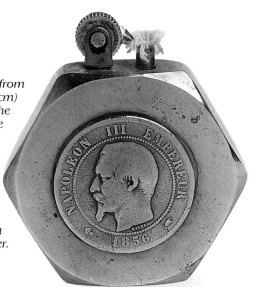

This lighter was made from a large 1¾-inch (4.6-cm) nut picked up on the battlefield. A gasoline reservoir has been created by plugging each side with an old coin on one side and a medallion representing three cherubs, a small girl, a lyre, and a violin on the other.

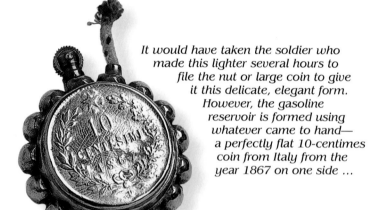

It would have taken the soldier who
made this lighter several hours to
file the nut or large coin to give
it this delicate, elegant form.
However, the gasoline
reservoir is formed using
whatever came to hand—
a perfectly flat 10-centimes
coin from Italy from the
year 1867 on one side ...

...and on the other, this highly ornate and beautifully curved button from a British army uniform. The final result is 1¼ inches (3.2 cm) wide and fairly heavy. Note that there is no snuff cap.

On this page and opposite
are both sides of the
same pocket lighter
with its belt ring and
hinged snuff cap.
One side of a steel
nut is sealed
by a silver coin
representing
the English Queen
Victoria (1819–1901),
George III's
granddaughter ...

...while the other side is decorated with another English silver coin, this time featuring George V (1865–1936). It was he who changed the name of the royal family from Saxe-Coburg to the more British name of Windsor. Note the 1911 tax mark soldered to the left side; it is no doubt recycled from a broken lighter.

A distinctive emblem of
the poilu from the 1914
war was his strangely
shaped flask, used
for water or wine,
depending on the
occasion. The flask
was reproduced in
miniature by a
number of soldiers,
and in this context
would contain gasoline.

Two factory-made flask shaped items. The larger one has a wick that is separate from the spark wheel. The wheel and flint cap are in this case removable, and are not shown here. To ignite the wick, the wheel is removed and sparked near the wick.

This proud Gallic rooster, symbol of the French nation, crows beneath the beaming sun and declares: "They will not pass! For Freedom's sake!" On the other side, there is an Alsatian dog, another much used and strong nationalist symbol of the disputed Alsace region.

This large piece of brass once held the bridle of a horse's harness. Its hollow form was used by poilus to manufacture lighters. It simply required sealing with a strip of brass punched with two holes to house the wick-holder and wheel cap. This lighter was made recently using recycled parts from the period.

With its three- (drei-) mark silver coin on one side, one might think that this lighter was made by a German soldier, but it may actually have been made by a French soldier using his spoils of war or a battlefield find. On the other side there is a copper coin of two centavos, the Argentinean currency.

Coins are useful in that they are dated and indicate a country's identity. Furthermore they are often made of quality metal. This penny coin, one of the least valuable of the British currency, is dated 1916. It is perfectly lodged in an eight-sided nut that has been filed down to produce this attractive six-sided piece.

*This crude lighter
was made from an empty
can of boot polish. It may not be the most attractive,
eye-catching model, and would probably not impress
high-society women in fashionable bars. However,
it must have been very precious to its maker
and friends, holed up in their barracks.*

This is a variation on the famous
caricature of the Crown Prince Wilhelm,
son of Kaiser Wilhelm II, and bugbear
of the French and English press.
The lighter is the work of a poilu
and is made in repoussé iron.
The inspiration for the design comes
from a combination of the enemy leader,
and from the character in a popular
illustrated series that began in 1908
and featured in the newspaper, L'Epatant.

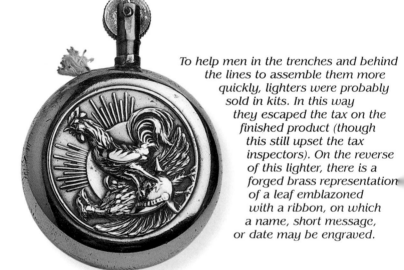

To help men in the trenches and behind
the lines to assemble them more
quickly, lighters were probably
sold in kits. In this way
they escaped the tax on the
finished product (though
this still upset the tax
inspectors). On the reverse
of this lighter, there is a
forged brass representation
of a leaf emblazoned
with a ribbon, on which
a name, short message,
or date may be engraved.

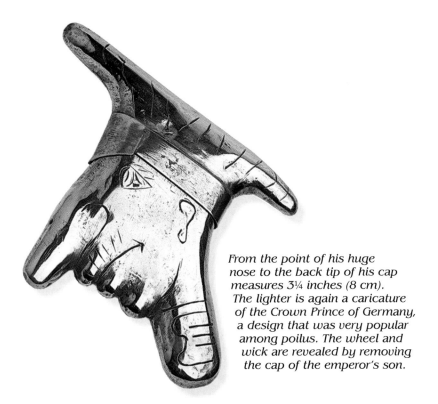

From the point of his huge
nose to the back tip of his cap
measures 3¼ inches (8 cm).
The lighter is again a caricature
of the Crown Prince of Germany,
a design that was very popular
among poilus. The wheel and
wick are revealed by removing
the cap of the emperor's son.

This is another poilu-made item, admirably fashioned using rudimentary tools, but executed with intelligence and taste. Firstly, a tube of copper was softened in the embers so that the craftsman could produce the desired curves. The nickel-plate finish to this gasoline lighter was no doubt added after the war.

The work of an experienced fitter, no doubt. This poilu lighter is a work of extraordinary precision, charm, and faith in reproduction. It is made of copper, brass, and recycled wood, and was fashioned with passion. Both photos of the leg opposite and the pistol are actual size.

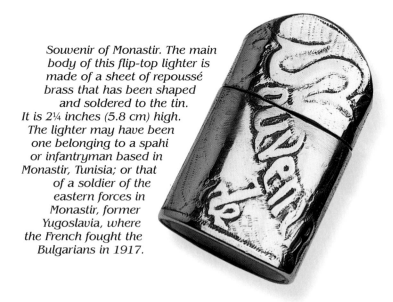

Souvenir of Monastir. The main body of this flip-top lighter is made of a sheet of repoussé brass that has been shaped and soldered to the tin. It is 2¼ inches (5.8 cm) high. The lighter may have been one belonging to a spahi or infantryman based in Monastir, Tunisia; or that of a soldier of the eastern forces in Monastir, former Yugoslavia, where the French fought the Bulgarians in 1917.

This souvenir of the Rhine, engraved by a soldier in the 1920s or 1930s is marked H.W. Patent 3. It opens automatically by pressing the button on the right. The spring makes the hinged top flip back, which gyrates the wheel and produces the sparks. Note the plug at the bottom enabling a gasoline refill.

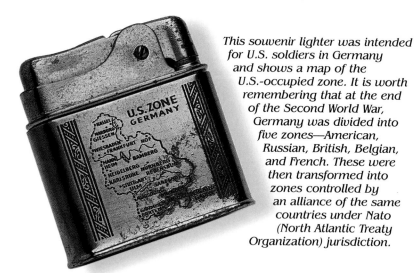

This souvenir lighter was intended for U.S. soldiers in Germany and shows a map of the U.S.-occupied zone. It is worth remembering that at the end of the Second World War, Germany was divided into five zones—American, Russian, British, Belgian, and French. These were then transformed into zones controlled by an alliance of the same countries under Nato (North Atlantic Treaty Organization) jurisdiction.

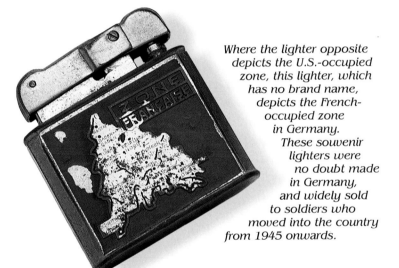

Where the lighter opposite depicts the U.S.-occupied zone, this lighter, which has no brand name, depicts the French-occupied zone in Germany.
These souvenir lighters were no doubt made in Germany, and widely sold to soldiers who moved into the country from 1945 onwards.

*This lighter is not a Zippo, but that did not stop
it ending up in Vietnam. It is a Japanese Penguin
lighter—a Zippo copy, though still of good quality.
The inscription on the reverse reads "Yosuka
An-Thoi Vung-Tau." The illustration selected by
its owner, Peter W. Hall, passes without comment.*

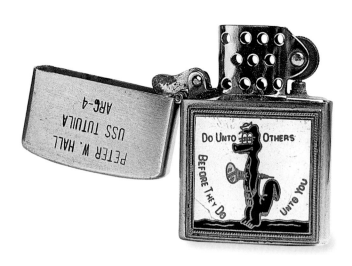

*In Italy as elsewhere, every warship had its own
lighter. This one from the Nave Lupo ("the Wolf
Ship") dates from 1987. On the other side is
the inscription "Swoop down on prey."*

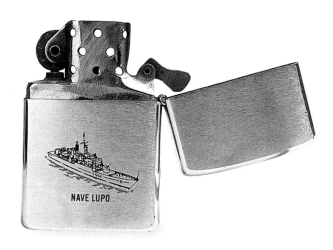

On the non-visible side of this lighter are the names Vietnam and Quinhon. It is dated 1968 and celebrates the Thirteenth Armored unit who chose Charles Schulz's Snoopy as their emblem.

*Every fresh war today produces new editions
of Zippo lighters. This camouflaged lighter
dates from January 1990 and commemorates
Desert Shield. There were others commemorating
the Desert Storm operation.*

The archetypal emblem of the Vietnamese
war—the Zippo—which was crudely
engraved by small electric machines
that were easy to operate.
The selected message was written
on a base and a small drill
engraved the letters
onto the metal.

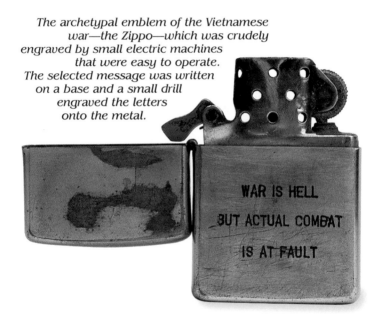

WAR IS HELL

BUT ACTUAL COMBAT

IS AT FAULT

This Zippo, featuring the dates 1967 and 1968, is a souvenir of a G.I.'s war years in the region around Cantho, South Vietnam. Again the selected emblem is that of Snoopy.

Quang Tri, as elsewhere in Vietnam, was a popular location for engraving Zippos. This lighter features the emblem of the elite parachute corps, the Eleventh Airborne. On the back of this lighter, dated 1968, is inscribed: "I know I'm going to heaven because I've lived in hell: Vietnam."

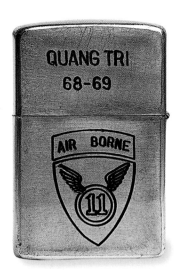

Dated 1966, this Zippo is another Vietnam remnant. It was sold by the army and its engraving is elaborate. The examples on the preceding pages are all hand-engraved or produced by crude local equipment.

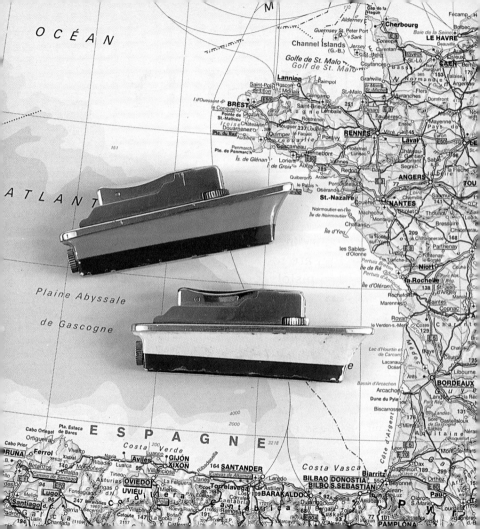

III

NOVELTY
lighters

This category includes keys that fit no lock, socks that are too small for any foot, assault tanks and pistols for pacifists, gasoline-fueled gasoline pumps, watches that do not tell the time, dogs that do not bark, and books without chapters. These are novelty lighters. They are made for their fun factor and surprise potential: lighters that can also captivate an audience. They are often unsigned works and come from sources as diverse as the trenches, the garage workshop, or the most highbrow business establishments.

Press the nose and this lighter opens. The faun's hair lifts up, and beneath it are the spark wheel and wick. The eyes are made of glass. There is no brand name.

The Manneken-Pis statue is the pride of Brussels, capital of Belgium, and the poor guy has turned up in all sorts of guises— as corkscrews, paper knives, and now as a lighter. The head unscrews to refill the gasoline, the wheel is on the left buttock, while the wick is beneath the vine leaf. It is not in the best of taste and is French-made. The original statue dates from 1619 and is the work of sculptor Jérôme Duquesnoy.

All poilu lighters are more or less figurative. This one is made from a watchcase that was no doubt picked off the battlefield. On the other side is a hunting scene featuring a bellowing stag.

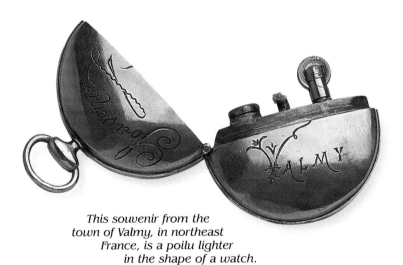

This souvenir from the town of Valmy, in northeast France, is a poilu lighter in the shape of a watch.

The base of this bottle-shaped lighter screws off to refill with the gasoline it needs for ignition. The upper section lifts off to reveal the spark wheel and wick.

This lighter is an ad for bottled cider produced in Normandy. The lighter has a wood finish and an imitation cork made of brass and iron wire. It is a gasoline lighter dating from about 1960.

Here is a large 4¾-inch (12-cm) wide faience lighter that contains another, much smaller but real lighter...

...There is therefore no point in pressing the visible mechanism to obtain a flame. It dates from the 1950s to 1960s, is covered in lizard skin, and functions on gasoline.

There are other book-shaped lighters in the section on soldiers' lighters. Here are another pair that are particularly well-made. The name of the owner, A. Chèze, is engraved on this one. The other one (facing page) is not engraved.

It would have taken an experienced poilu about two hours to make a simple model such as this.

This type of lighter was widespread during the 1960s and 1970s and was on sale in almost all tobacconists. The lighter mechanism itself is on top of the tank's turret.

The Jeep was one of the symbols of the Liberation of France at the end of the Second World War. A number of surprising souvenirs were based on it. One is this smoker's kit including cigarette holder (beneath the roof), a lighter (beneath the hood), and a trailer-ashtray. It was made by Bauer in Germany in the U.S.-occupied zone at the end of the 1940s.

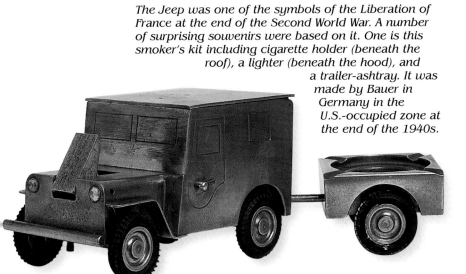

To have a souvenir wooden gasoline lighter from the Algerian capital, Algiers, in the shape of a champagne cork is quite surprising. This series would have celebrated other towns, no doubt equally far away from the exclusive champagne production region in the northeast of France.

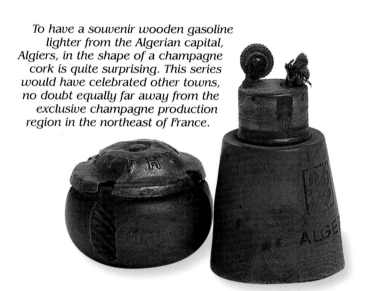

This unusual table lighter is the wooden sculpture of a dog. Its mechanism is revealed by tipping back the animal's head. It is gasoline-fueled and carries no brand name. It dates from the 1950s.

*The die is considered a symbol of luck in
some Western countries. These three handbag
lighters work with butane, bear the Ippag
brand, and date from the 1960s.*

This die-shaped lighter is larger and functions on gasoline. It is made of chrome-plated steel, and dates, like those on the facing page, from the 1960s. No brand name.

*This lighter was made using a Mauser bullet from
the First World War, as well as a spark wheel from the
period, an old key, and a tax mark taken from the body
of an old lighter. This model is not authentic, however.
The materials are indeed antique, but it was actually
constructed at the end of the twentieth century.*

*Lighters come in all shapes and sizes.
So why not also use the shape of a key as well,
and then it can be attached to a key ring? The one
at the top is of the French Myon brand, the two below
are American, made by Lucky Key. The gasoline reservoir
is in the chrome-plated nickel shaft.*

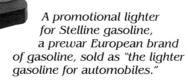

*A promotional lighter
for Stelline gasoline,
a prewar European brand
of gasoline, sold as "the lighter
gasoline for automobiles."*

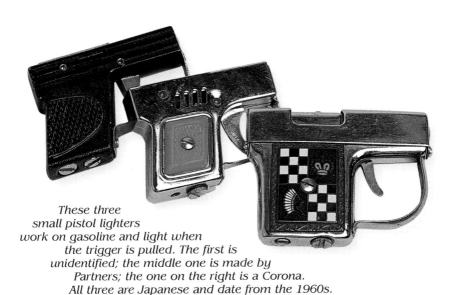

*These three
small pistol lighters
work on gasoline and light when
the trigger is pulled. The first is
unidentified; the middle one is made by
Partners; the one on the right is a Corona.
All three are Japanese and date from the 1960s.*

As when
loading some
real pistols,
here the barrel
slides across. The motion reveals
the wick, a necessary step before lighting. Note the
French tax mark, which means that this gasoline
lighter dates from before 1945.

The "Jym" must
have caused
a riot during
the dances
of the 1950s—
or certainly raised
a few eyebrows.
Which was probably
just what the manufacturer
of this Bakelite gasoline lighter
was after. It takes so little
to have a fine old time.

Unlike the combined camera and lighter on page 239, which is capable of both functions, this "camera" is in fact just a lighter. To obtain a flame, simply press the shutter of this Japanese-made K.K.W. Camera Lighter.

On the base of this tiny gasoline lighter (just 1½ inches [3.7-cm] wide), shaped like a camera, is the inscription: "Made in occupied Japan," which dates it to around 1948.

A "striker lighter" from 1920s Germany, with the friction strip on the top of the shoe. The ball lifts off to allow the gasoline reservoir to be refilled, and to remove the match with its steel tip. DRGM are the German Empire initials indicating a government patent without quality guarantee.

This clodhopper made of recycled nickel and copper is a particularly tricky number to create and was made by the deftest of poilus. Note the care paid to each and every detail, like the little repair patch near the base. When the boot is turned over, the nails can be seen, stamped in one by one; the sole has not even been soldered.

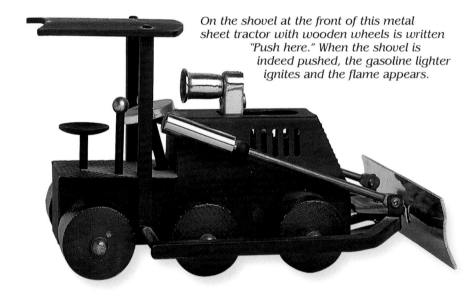

On the shovel at the front of this metal sheet tractor with wooden wheels is written *"Push here."* When the shovel is indeed pushed, the gasoline lighter ignites and the flame appears.

Like the lighter in the shape of the assault tank on page 192, this 5¾-inch (14.5-cm) high lantern functions on butane and is not perhaps the most interesting of firelighting examples. It is worth showing that such objects do exist, however.

Contrary to popular belief, the jerry can is in fact a German invention. "Jerry" was the name given to German soldiers; by transferring the name to the can, Americans have paid a kind of homage to its makers. Here the lighter is also made by the Jerrican brand.

Another lighter shaped like a jerry can, this time from Japan, where the name is patented as a manufacturer's brand. This lighter also works on gasoline and has borrowed the Zippo flip-top idea.

The heart, the symbol of love, has been turned
to many uses and appears in many forms
all over the world. This lighter dates
from the 1930s and functions
on gasoline. It may be
worn as jewelry.

This copper heart is not factory-finished and was made by a poilu. The gasoline reservoir fills by lifting the lighter flint cap.

*The head
covering the wick lifts off here
to ignite this short-haired dachshund.
It measures 4 inches (10 cm) long from
the end of the nose to the tip of the tail.
It is made of pewter and dates from the 1920s.*

To open this fish-shaped lighter— a carp, no doubt—the head is removed to reveal the spark wheel and wick system. Made of copper and nickel. Possibly a poilu's work.

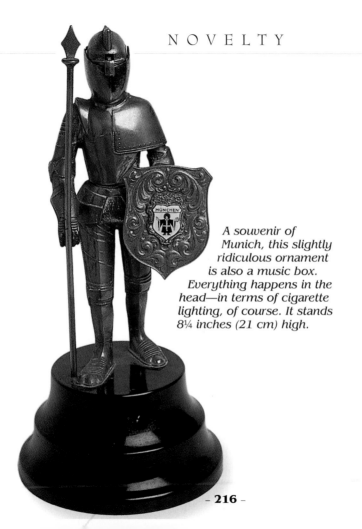

A souvenir of Munich, this slightly ridiculous ornament is also a music box. Everything happens in the head—in terms of cigarette lighting, of course. It stands 8¼ inches (21 cm) high.

This other knight
in armor works on
gasoline, as does
the one on the facing
page. The spark
wheel is in the visor
and the soaked wick
reacts to the sparks.
It is 7½ inches
(19.5 cm) high.

*The first submarines went into service during
the First World War and had a big effect
on people's imaginations. It is not surprising
that a number of poilus reproduced them
in recycled nickel and copper.*

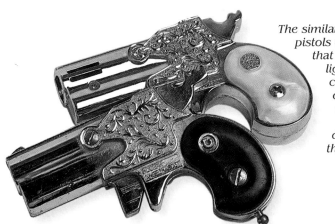

The similarities between pistols or revolvers that are fired and lighters that create fire have often been exploited. This pair dates from the 1970s.

A butane lighter in the shape of a P38 revolver, here on its original wooden support. The flame is produced at the end of the barrel.

*Where the lighter on the left works on butane,
this one functions on gasoline. Notice the tip of the flint
shaft on the right. The lighter is refilled via the barrel
of the gun. Both date back to the 1970s and 1980s.
It is plain to see how bad taste develops over time,
when we compare these lighters to those made fifty,
sixty, or seventy years earlier.*

This might look like a pen but it is actually a lighter that works like a "striker lighter." Below, there is the ferrocerium plate that serves as a friction strip. The steel silver rod with its gasoline-soaked wick is stored (screwed) in the top of this pen-lighter. Made by Ronson, U.S.A., 1919.

*This poilu lighter is a tube of stretched nickel in the shape
of a trumpet. It is doubtless the work of a First World War
musician. Its gasoline capacity is fairly limited.*

A trompe-l'oeil lighter from the end of the 1940s or the start of the 1950s, made by Kaschlie. After this name can be read, "Made in Germany, U.S. zone," which besides locating its manufacture, helps greatly to date it, too. To light this gasoline lighter, the finger is introduced in the candlestick handle then the lever above pressed with the thumb. These operations trigger the opening of the dome of the imitation candle above, allowing the flame to appear. Dunhill produced a similar model.

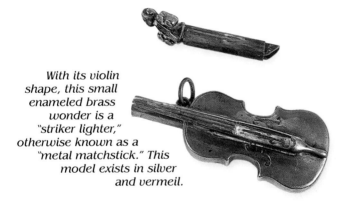

With its violin shape, this small enameled brass wonder is a "striker lighter," otherwise known as a "metal matchstick." This model exists in silver and vermeil.

The fashion for cordless telephones—before the invention of the cellular phone—engendered several lighters. This one is Chinese and made at the end of the 1980s.

This one seems to bear a striking resemblance to the former French president, Charles de Gaulle. Or it could be a French traffic cop. Made of turned aluminum, the lighter separates at the belt line.

IV

LUXURY
lighters

No sooner had the first gasoline lighter—
with its spark wheel and wick—left the
drawing board than it was snapped up
by the top jewelers and treated as a gem.
At the bottom of the range there are silver alloys,
then solid silver, gold, and vermeil for more
expensive tastes. The luxury lighter bears the
hallmarks of prestige—Boucheron, Hermès,
Dunhill, Cartier, Lancel, and S.T. Dupont, the French
designer who started a lighter range in the 1940s,
refining it over time, and whose products became
highly fashionable twenty years later.

*This trompe l'oeil
lighter is made by Dunhill and called
the "Tinder Pistol," patent 592139.
It was marketed until the 1950s and
resembles the first flint lighters, but actually
works on gasoline, which is ignited by a spark
wheel fitted with an Auer flint.*

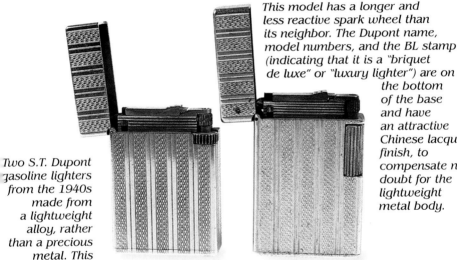

This model has a longer and less reactive spark wheel than its neighbor. The Dupont name, model numbers, and the BL stamp (indicating that it is a "briquet de luxe" or "luxury lighter") are on the bottom of the base and have an attractive Chinese lacquer finish, to compensate no doubt for the lightweight metal body.

Two S.T. Dupont gasoline lighters from the 1940s made from a lightweight alloy, rather than a precious metal. This model measures 2 inches (5 cm) high.

*In 1939 S.T. Dupont,
a leather designer,
conceived of a gold lighter
similar in shape to the
Dunhill, which he produced
for the Maharajah of Patiala.
This simpler model has
a barley finish and dates
from the same period.*

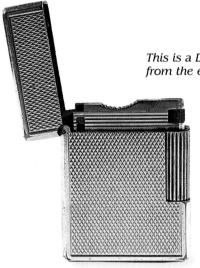

This is a Dupont gasoline lighter from the end of the 1940s. It is silver-plated, but also exists in solid silver. Notice the notched switch on top that draws the unit back to change the flint. This switch unit is newer than its counterpart on the left and is clearly a replacement.

This peculiar gasoline lighter was made by Flamidor, Paris. It has a crystal body and a small ring for hanging or attaching to a chain. It could be a handbag lighter, or might have been worn as a piece of jewelry like....

... the bracelet on this page. The butterfly wings are made of galalith, a hard plastic made of milk casein solidified using formaldehyde. The name comes from the Greek gala *(milk)* and lithos *(stone).* Both these gasoline lighters were made by Flamidor and date from the 1930s or 1940s.

Mellerio dits Meller are very Parisian jewelers, though originally from Italy. They founded their establishment in 1750. In 1952, their boutique was situated on the prestigious rue de la Paix, the jewelers' quarter in Paris, and this superb silver gasoline lighter, decorated with diagonal streaks, was one of their gems.

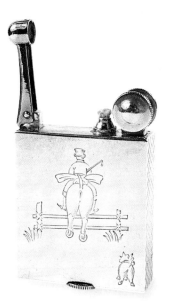

This is the same lighter as on the facing page, but this side has a much less elegant design. The reason for this is simple. This particular model was carried by Mellerio salesmen in their valise. To avoid filling their showcase up with extra weight, the same lighter would feature two very different designs.

"Echo 8" is a real lighter, but it is also a fully working camera. The lighter itself works with gasoline and its white metal exterior imitates silver well. The camera uses a 16-mm film cut in two along its length, hence the name Echo 8. The small notched wheel winds the film on and switches from one shot to the next. There is also an ASA dial and f-stop. The viewfinder is the small square in the flip-top. This is a true spy camera made in the U.S. during the 1930s and 1940s.

Even the workingman's Zippo gasoline lighter can dress up chic. This is a ten-carat gold-plated "Slim" model, from 1961.

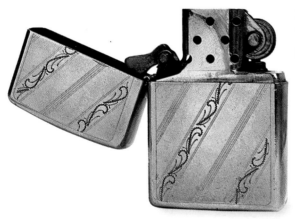

This "Regular" Zippo is also more upmarket with its silver plate. Like the earlier Zippo models made in the 1930s, its base is flat. Clues to its date are obvious: the base is marked with "L" and "VIII," which denotes December 1992.

*This unused Zippo
still bears its price
in dollars. It is the
"Scrimshaw Ship"
model, no. 359.
It is dated 1986
and has no engraving
on the other side.*

This Zippo table lighter is called "The Corinthian." It was manufactured between early 1960 and the end of 1966 based on the feminine "Slim" Zippo design. It cost $16.50 and came in three colors—gray, white, and turquoise.

"Abdulla" is one of Marcel Quercia's brands. Quercia,
as well as inventing the butane lighter, has contributed
much to the world of lighters. This automatic gasoline
model dates from the 1930s and has a lacquer
and eggshell design. The metal parts are simply gilded.
The spark wheel, top right, is safer for pocket use.
The other notched wheel, bottom left, adjusts
the tension of the spring pushing the flint.

The Dunhill "Circle" is one of the most elegant lighters of the series, and its round form makes it pocket-friendlier. It dates from the end of the 1920s and was manufactured for ten years. This silver-plated gasoline model was also sold with a watch.

What is surprising about this silver gasoline lighter from the 1930s is that its rear panel slides out for refueling, so avoiding unsightly fill screws. This is a British-made Dunhill "Back."

This 8-inch (20-cm) long Victorian table lighter works with a mercury fulminate spark wheel, as Baron Auer's flint had not yet been invented. To create sparks, the two handles were pinched together to ignite a small hemispherical candle surrounded by a phosphorus amalgam.
Patented B & AB.

This very attractive solid silver gasoline lighter was created by Cartier at the end of the 1920s or start of the 1930s. There was also a gold and Chinese lacquer and gold version as well as one incrusted with precious stones. It is 2½ inches (6.5 cm) high and was marketed by Dunhill as the "Tall Boy," under the Cartier license.

This fairly simple model is decorated with an Ecorce, or "bark" motif, created by the jeweler Boucheron, another example of which is on page 276. This flint and tinder-wick lighter is made of solid gold and silver and was marketed during the 1940s, a period of great energy shortages.

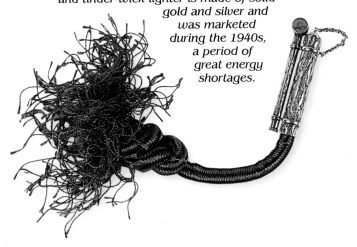

Silver desk lighter made in the 1940s by Aucoc, whose jewelry outlet was in the prestigious quarter of rue de la Paix in Paris.

Dunhill "Savory" gasoline lighter, manufactured in Switzerland, as it featured in the Dunhill catalog in 1950. It was also produced in a lacquered version designed by the writing instrument designer, Namiki. The G.K. initials here are those of the former owner.

This automatic gasoline pocket lighter with sun motif was produced by the German firm Pilot from the 1930s to 1955.

*Another Art Deco
sun motif, this time
made by a jeweler.
This is a Dunhill
butane lighter.*

*Whether designed for pocket or table, butane
lighters from the 1950s to the 1970s provide
inexhaustible and fascinating research subjects
and cause constant surprise; there were many
produced around the world. They provide a good
introduction to the subject for the keen debutant
collector who has a limited budget.*

Jazz music made its appearance in Europe in 1917, introduced by the American troops. It set up shop in the years after the end of the First World War. Polaire followed the fashion with this attractive gasoline table lighter featuring a saxophone player.

This is an upmarket version of the Flaminaire lighter from the start of the 1950s, in its original box. It is made of solid silver and has a renewable butane canister, which, once empty, was swapped at the tobacconist's and returned to the factory for refilling. This was then sent back to the tobacconist's for collection by the owner.

In 1918, Ryosuke Namiki founded Pilot, his writing equipment company, and from 1925 onward, started producing pens decorated with scenes of nature using the traditional Maki-e Japanese lacquer technique. His motifs were plated in gold and silver. Fashion caught up with this process and Dunhill followed suit with this "Square Boy" lighter.

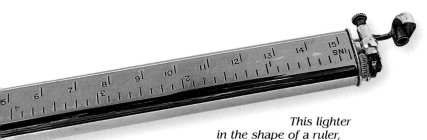

*This lighter
in the shape of a ruler,
marked with centimeters and inches,
is one of the last gasoline lighters that Dunhill
produced. It is made of silver-plated metal
and dates from the 1950s. Known as the
"Sylph Ruler," there was a variation on
the form with a paper cutter at the end.*

The first model of this Dunhill lighter dates from 1934. This ruler is one-foot long. The "Architect" model, however, is a full yard long. Sometimes, you have to go to great lengths to refuel a lighter.

*As a rule, an object that is beautiful will soon be
copied. In the case of lighters, Dunhill's models have
been frequently imitated. On this page and facing are
two examples of lighter piracy. Here is a copy of
the "Foot-Rule" model created by Alfred Dunhill.*

*The model on the facing
page (made by SCLR)
is gasoline-fueled.
This Dunhill copy,
inspired from
the "Sylphide" model,
runs on propane.*

During the period of French colonization, the Myon brand, belonging to Marcel Quercia, produced a number of different table lighters featuring motifs from French protectorates or other far-flung territories. This silver "Indochina" model, with its dragon illustrations, appeared during the 1930s...

...as did this one,
evoking Cambodia.
There were also lighters
dedicated to Algeria,
Tunisia, Morocco,
and East and West
African colonies.

This Dunhill "Vanity" model may look like a lighter,
but do not be fooled. Made in 1920, by the famous
British jewelers, it is a trompe l'oeil...

...containing a tube of lipstick, face powder and a small mirror—everything necessary to prepare for a date. It is one silver lighter that is for non-smokers only.

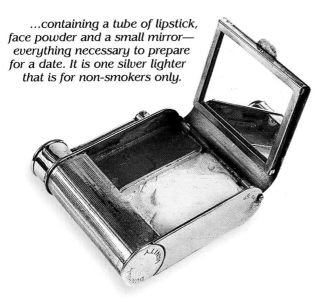

Celluloid designs were very popular for table lighters, as for many other objects, at the end of the 1920s. Celluloid was invented by two Americans, the Hyatt brothers, and introduced into Europe at the end of the nineteenth century. It is a synthetic product obtained from nitric cellulose, which is plasticized using camphor.

This Japanese pocket gasoline lighter,
from the 1950s, is a Ronson copy and may
be easily mistaken for the real article.

Its base is so heavy that all that is needed to trigger the ignition mechanism of this table lighter is to lift its body. It was made in Germany of enameled nickel.

The design of this Swiss gasoline table lighter was based on the aerodynamic automobiles of the 1930s, and was manufactured prior to and after the war. A musical version was also produced.

The brand is unknown, but this candlestick-shaped lighter comes from Germany. It is fueled on gasoline and its base, fitted with two cigarette-rests, operates as an ashtray. It stands 5 inches (13 cm) high.

This attractive gasoline lighter is automatic. The trigger is on the left of the mechanism. A lighter is said to be "automatic" if it uncovers the wick and spins the spark wheel, in one action, without an extra thumb flick.

An appealing automatic Lancel desk lighter with an elegant cross-ruled diamond point design. This one is silver-plated. The model also came in a gold-plated version.

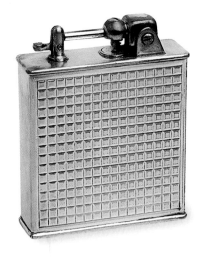

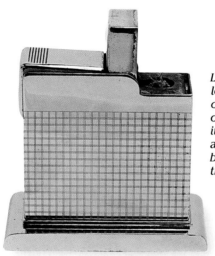

Like its neighbor on the left, this table lighter dates from the end of the 1930s. With its fitted hood, it was a style that would become all the rage in the 1950s. It is 3 inches (7.6 cm) high, and was made by Conly.

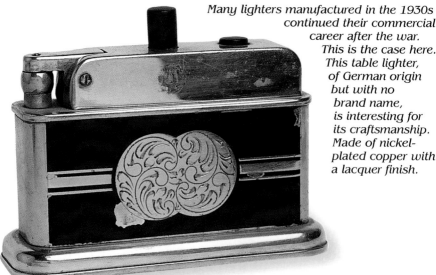

Many lighters manufactured in the 1930s continued their commercial career after the war. This is the case here. This table lighter, of German origin but with no brand name, is interesting for its craftsmanship. Made of nickel-plated copper with a lacquer finish.

This classic pre-war Polaire model comes in chrome-plated brass and measures 4 inches (10 cm) high. A similar model is fitted with a watch.

The jeweler Boucheron adapted his Ecorce or "bark" textured motif for a "Slim" Zippo lighter—the slightest of models, targeted at a female market. This model came in solid silver or gold.

Here in the base of this lighter clock is a fine example of the charms of old zamac as it disintegrates. Zamac stands for Zinc Aluminum Magnesium Antimony, and Copper, its component parts. This chrome-plated and lacquered gasoline model dates from the 1930s. It is made by Polaire and measures 4¾ inches (12.2 cm) high.

Automatic gasoline-fueled desk or table lighters, in this case a Lancel, are identifiable by the small switch on the far right. Simply press this switch and the flame appears. Imagine such a mechanism without any other safeguard in a pocket or at the bottom of a handbag.

To reveal the mechanism and ignite this lighter, the button in the middle must be pushed up. This model is made by Etna, with its downward pointing triangle logo, in Italy, around 1935. This particular version was sold in France between the two wars and features the French government tax stamp.

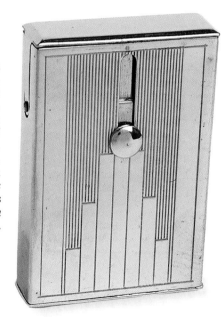

*On the whole, this lighter would
be fairly commonplace, but for
the attractive mother-of-pearl case
which makes it much more
appealing. It is a gasoline lighter
from around 1940.*

Made of silver-plated metal and covered with lizard skin, this is a "Vulcano", patent number 44185. Collectors tend to find that a large number of this type and make feature military insignia; many of these lighters were produced specifically for the military.

This superb Lancel table lighter was made and patented in France. This one dates from 1927, but other versions exist. The marking underneath helps date these lighters.

This is a very rare lighter with a friction strip, dating from the beginning of the Roaring Twenties. Women could keep such a lighter in their handbags on a small chain or attached to a bracelet as jewelry. This one is in gold and Chinese lacquer.

This gasoline lighter displays its jeweler's remarkable design work. It is made by Marin, a goldsmith located on the rue du Faubourg-Saint-Honoré in Paris. It is made of silver and gold, inset with rubies. The leather-clad presentation case in which the lighter was sold is also a rare item.

This lighter bears the name of Unis France and is indeed a Flamidor, with an SGDG patent—without government quality guarantee. Unis France was a bulk-buying group rather than the actual manufacturer. This is an automatic gasoline model with a leather and tortoiseshell cover. It exists in several sizes, from pocket to desk forms.

This small gilded handbag lighter is encased in crocodile skin. Note its hard protective case, which prevents it opening unexpectedly and thereby causing damage to the contents of a handbag.

This Flamidor from the 1920s is covered in pink shagreen. It is a table lighter, measuring 2¾ inches (7 cm) high, with a distinctive steel spark wheel. Such spark wheels are useful when it comes to dating old lighters.

In collectors' jargon, these Dunhill lighters are said to be "double wheels," because there are two separate spark wheels to light the wick. There is a steel one that sparks the ferrocerium flint, and the silver one for the thumb to flick. To begin with, Dunhill only included one wheel to fulfill both of these functions. These are called "single wheel" lighters.

Dunhill lighters came in three sizes, A, B and C, from the smallest to the largest. The volume of the lighter body did not affect size classification. Here are two B models.

This handsome Mouchon-license Racer 75-17 gasoline lighter has to be pressed on both sides to obtain a flame. It is made of solid silver and Chinese lacquer and is 1¾ inches (4.8 cm) high.

The original cap and the refined oval form of this 1930s lighter seem to have been carefully produced. It is in fact a fake luxury lighter. Its appearance is acceptable, but it is lightweight and, when used, betrays a number of other less luxurious attributes.

This is a classic attractive
dual function lighter made
by Swiss producers Listen.
The winder of the watch
is on the right.

Again a model inspired by the famous Dunhill lighter of the end of the 1920s. The floral motif here is unusually well executed. The watch's winder is invisible and the lighter has to be opened, using the clip in the center, to access the watch.

The winder of this watch, used also to change the time, is very discreet and well integrated into the whole. It is at the bottom of the lighter. This attractive model was made by Eterna in the 1930s and is covered in snakeskin.

*This example is perhaps less chic
than the version on the left, but
it still tells the time accurately.
This dual function model was
widespread in the U.S.*

Generally lighter makers import the watches installed on their products. Here the opposite has happened. Eterna is first and foremost a Swiss watchmaker with a great reputation. The firm even devised another model that wound the watch when the cover at the top was lifted.

This small gasoline-fueled lighter, produced by a jeweler for handbag use or for traveling, is a remarkable model, made in gold with Chinese lacquer finish. Around 1930.

Alfred Dunhill lighters were so sought after that many manufacturers copied them or adapted their designs. One such is this small pocket model covered in celluloid and dating from the 1920s or 1930s.

These two interesting lighters can be picked up at flea markets. On the left is a good Dunhill copy and, on the right, a Myon 201. The latter is fairly plain but its silver motif lifts it out of the ordinary. Furthermore, the inside section can be removed to reveal a map of Indochina.

This is the famous Dunhill "Squareboy"
lighter, first sold in 1937. Its name
came from its elegant square
shape. It was available in
different metals—gold
and silver-plated,
or solid silver.

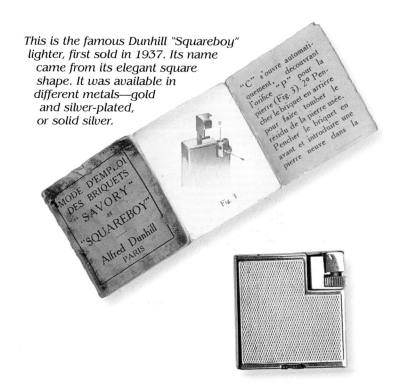

This is a large, "luxury style" gasoline-fueled table lighter from the 1930s. It is in fact a factory-made model in the image of the Fujiyama lighters, which were actually a French brand, despite the Japanese name.

A straightforward
Flaminaire, the original
butane lighter can take
on a different complexion
when silver-plated, as with
this "Crillon" model which,
from 1947 onwards, sold
hundreds of thousands.

This is a handsome
Dunhill pocket
butane lighter.
Its case is in vermeil
and gold and it was
marketed under the
name of "Sylphide."
It dates from around
1960 and was
produced for a good
ten years using
precious metals.

This lighter was baptized the "Salaam." It is a gasoline-fueled Dunhill from immediately after the war. This model has an anodized finish, but several rare others have a Japanese lacquer finish with different motifs.

In the Dunhill catalogues at the end of the 1920s, this pair of gasoline lighters were dubbed "Unic Bijou." The name "bijou" referred to the petite size of these little wonders. They came in silver or gold. The one on the right is a "Unic Bijou Sport" and the wick cover (that can be seen page 289 on another Dunhill) has been removed.

With its gadroons
and smooth shields,
this Cartier lighter,
made in Paris, has
seen some action.
Note the quarter-
circle hook that
guides the cap
back into place.

The name of the Dunhill "Sport" comes from its flame shield, the openwork designed accessory that prevents the flame from blowing out in high winds—while golfing or fishing, for example.

A metal alloy company,
SAM, situated in the Marais
in Paris, has produced
materials for the greats
such as Chaumet and
Hermès. This silver lighter
with gold incrustations was
made by Chaumet,
the famous jeweler
of Paris's Place Vendôme.

Dating from the 1930s, this model is a very chic pocket gasoline lighter produced by Lancel. It is made of solid silver and has an automatic mechanism. Note the engraved initials, L.B., of its owner.

*Gasoline lighter from
the 1930s which,
despite being 70 years
old, is as good as new.
It is made of enameled
vermeil in a Russian
style. Its manufacturer,
Rex, is French.*

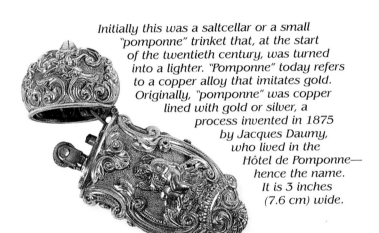

Initially this was a saltcellar or a small
"pomponne" trinket that, at the start
of the twentieth century, was turned
into a lighter. "Pomponne" today refers
to a copper alloy that imitates gold.
Originally, "pomponne" was copper
lined with gold or silver, a
process invented in 1875
by Jacques Daumy,
who lived in the
Hôtel de Pomponne—
hence the name.
It is 3 inches
(7.6 cm) wide.

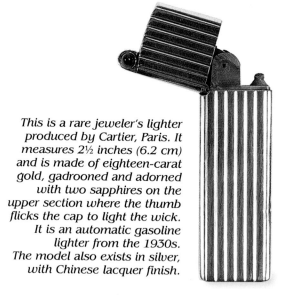

This is a rare jeweler's lighter produced by Cartier, Paris. It measures 2½ inches (6.2 cm) and is made of eighteen-carat gold, gadrooned and adorned with two sapphires on the upper section where the thumb flicks the cap to light the wick. It is an automatic gasoline lighter from the 1930s. The model also exists in silver, with Chinese lacquer finish.

This small 1¾-inch (4.5-cm) long lighter is a gasoline-fueled "striker lighter" for elegant ladies or dandies. It is in lacquered silver and has a carry ring. The match, also in silver, rubs against the ferrocerium strip along the body of the lighter opposite the ring. It was made around 1920.

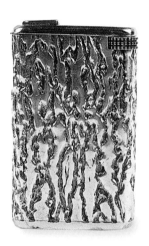

The jeweler
Boucheron created
the Ecorce or "bark"
textured motif on
this butane lighter
using the lighting
system from 1950s
Feudor lighters.
It is made of
silver and gold.

The small wheel, left, is used to adjust the pressure on the flint, which enhances user comfort. It is gasoline-fueled and dates from the 1930s. It is an intermediary size between the pocket and desk lighter.

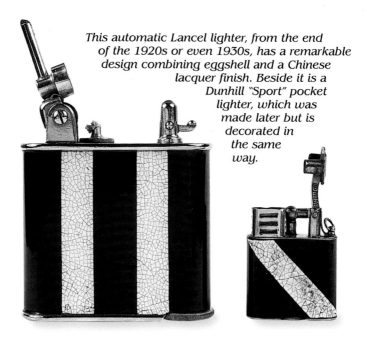

This automatic Lancel lighter, from the end of the 1920s or even 1930s, has a remarkable design combining eggshell and a Chinese lacquer finish. Beside it is a Dunhill "Sport" pocket lighter, which was made later but is decorated in the same way.

This example is more an alarm clock than a lighter. The handsome Lancel automatic table model in polished brass is gasoline-fueled and includes an eight-day clock as well as showing the days of the week. By simply pressing the switch top right, the lighter ignites.

Marcel Quercia invented the butane lighter in 1948. His "trilogy" consists of the "Gentry," "Baronet," and "Crillon" models. The trio was first introduced to the public at a presentation at the prestigious Hôtel de Crillon in Paris. Here is an example of a "Crillon" lighter with its Ecorce finish, designed by the jeweler Boucheron.

This automatic flameless lighter has a chrome-plated brass case and, in profile, resembles an airplane wing. The mechanism inside is beautifully polished. This is an American model from the 1940s, made by the Lektrolite Corporation and bearing the patent number 2.005.476.

This automatic gasoline lighter from Lancel came in several different finishes. Here it is covered in shagreen, but was also available in snake—or lizard—skin. The first automatic lighters did not have an interrupter, which meant that the flint wore down more easily, not only when the spring was triggered, but also when shutting down the system.

*This Abdulla automatic with protective screen shields
the flame from the wind. It is also equipped with
a security wheel (top right), enabling closure
of the lighter so that it can be slipped into a pocket
or handbag. The finish here is enamel
and it dates from the 1930s.*

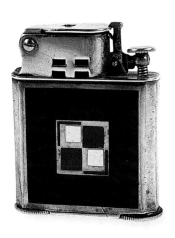

The French painter and printmaker Bernard Buffet decorated this "Galet" (or "pebble") model for Flaminaire in the 1950s. He was not the only creator to work for the company, and they also marketed a limited series of Pablo Picasso lighters.

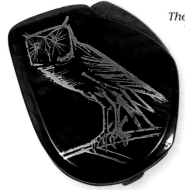

The reverse side of the "Galet" on the facing page features an owl drawn with straight lines—typical of Bernard Buffet's work. Buffet was born in 1928 and died in 1999. The "Galet" model also came in gold and silver.

At the start of the 1950s,
the Italian aperitif producer,
Cinzano, based a promotional
campaign on men's leisure
pursuits. Fishing and
trapshooting competitions
featured prizes with Cinzano
motifs. It seems that this
engraved lighter, dubbed
"The Gold Cartridge," and made
by the goldsmith Bancelin,
was one such prize. It is made
of vermeil and was based on
the Crillon lighter (page 318).

This lighter is part of the "Galet" series, another example of which is on the preceding double page. This is not a pocket lighter, but a table version. It contains lead to give it poise and weight. It dates from around 1960 and is butane-fueled.

V

PROMOTIONAL
lighters

A longside the tried and true key ring, the lighter is another marketing gadget that has come a long way. The idea of stamping initials, a slogan, or an image on a lighter to make the recipient think about the source of the gift every time it is used is an old trick. This form of publicity worked particularly well in the United States where, from 1932 onward, George Grant Blaisdell developed the Zippo, a gasoline lighter built to resist a storm. Its two plain sides lent themselves marvelously to the addition of promotional symbols.

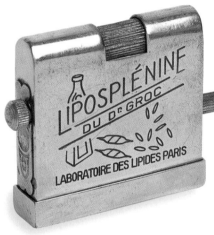

This strange contraption was, despite its appearance, indeed an automatic gasoline lighter from between the two wars. To light it, the cover was removed to reveal the striated top section before pressing the button on the right. Here the ad is for a health tonic, Liposplénine, produced by the mysterious "Doctor Groc."

During the ascendancy of disposable lighters, many forms were tried. This fake plastic matchbox is one such experiment. The smoker merely had to press the button on the side to obtain a flame from the hole in the top. Here the slogan reads, Growing up is Nestlé."

The manufacturer's name does not feature on this lighter, but we know it comes from Japan. It was distributed in outlets stocking Levi-Strauss denim jeans. From the start of the 1960s onwards, this form of lighter, as we shall see, was chosen for a number of advertisements. The reverse side of this model is featured bottom left on page 326.

A chrome-plated metal lighter stamped with "Made in France." It is an ad for SAF, a company specializing in smoking accessories in the 1930s.

To recharge this Rowenta gasoline lighter, the whole mechanism lifts out. The model featured a number of different motifs— in this case, a map of Switzerland. Around 1965.

Promotional table lighter for Sanz furniture.
It functions on butane, the flame being produced
by the small button below.
It measures 4¼ inches (11 cm) wide.

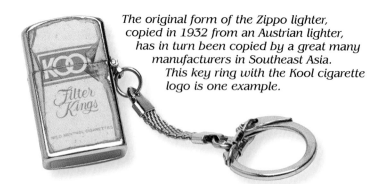

The original form of the Zippo lighter,
copied in 1932 from an Austrian lighter,
has in turn been copied by a great many
manufacturers in Southeast Asia.
This key ring with the Kool cigarette
logo is one example.

This slightly worn example is an ad for a German company, Jurid, a manufacturer of joints and spare parts for automobiles.

*These two interesting gasoline
lighters are both based on the same theme—
that of the storage bag.
The Poliet & Chausson company sold
construction materials in just such
a packaging. Around 1960.*

*The firm Michelin,
based in Central France,
simply had to dig into its bag of
primary materials to find the design for
this promotional lighter made from an inner tube
valve. The idea came from the poilus—frontline soldiers—
of 1914, who produced similar models.*

French automobile manufacturers, Ballot Automobiles, existed from 1919 to 1931. Already in 1905, Edouard and Maurice Ballot were building boat engines. This explains the anchor on their logo. The government tax mark is visible on the bottom of the lighter. It measures 1½ inches (4 cm) in diameter.

We stay in the world of the automobile with these two oilcan-shaped lighters—firstly Esso, a company started by J.D. Rockefeller at the end of the nineteenth century, and then, Igol, a French brand created in 1949. Finally, the third lighter on the right is French, promoting an American tractor constructor, International Harvester. All are gasoline lighters from the 1960s and 1970s.

This is an all American
lighter, the "Wonderliter,"
advertising Chevrolet—
which was actually
founded by a Swiss
adventurer, Louis Chevrolet.
This gasoline model is a
"striker lighter" that needs
unscrewing (on top).
The friction strip is on
the base of the lighter.

This imposing promotional lighter for the Ripolin brand of paint is actually only 4¾ inches (12 cm) high. It is destined for the table, or maybe the counter of a hardware store.

Beer-producers take a great deal of interest in smokers and distribute matchboxes, pyrogenic products, and lighters. This is a lighter that is shaped like a bottle of Grünhall, a German beer.

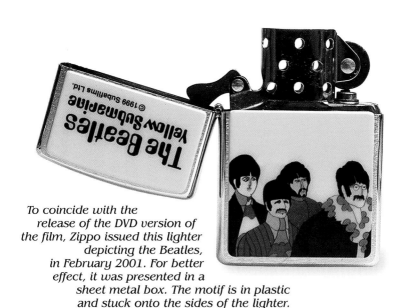

To coincide with the release of the DVD version of the film, Zippo issued this lighter depicting the Beatles, in February 2001. For better effect, it was presented in a sheet metal box. The motif is in plastic and stuck onto the sides of the lighter.

There are an infinite number of lighters to collect if one is also open to other areas, such as the movies. Here is a collection of disposable Bic lighters, celebrating novelist Ian Fleming and his character James Bond.

These small promotional lighters, shaped like tubes of lipstick, have various different brand logos marked on them, such as that of the mineral-water producer, Evian. The low-cost model appealed to other sponsors advertising a multitude of products. This is another good starting point for a novice amateur collector on a low budget.

In profile, when the brand name is hidden, it is not easy to tell a real Zippo from a copy. In your opinion, is this lighter with the words "Swing Time" splashed across it "made in Bradford, U.S.A.," or not? The answer is no. It is a copy manufactured by Champ.

This lighter is a souvenir of Lübeck, a German port of the Schleswig-Holstein region in the north of Germany. It is a gasoline model, made by KW, in chrome-plated brass, dating from the 1950s.

In its small cardboard box marked Japan on the back, this model is a Penguin Superlative Automatic Lighter, no. 18250. Pepsi was created in 1896 by Caleb Bradham.

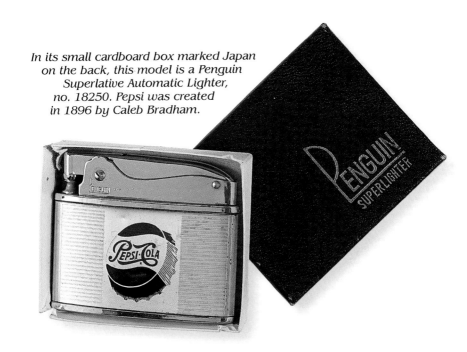

*These promotional gasoline lighters for Dunlop tires
come in tire shapes. It was John Boyd Dunlop,
a veterinary surgeon, who invented pneumatic tires.
He thought the solid rubber tires on his son's tricycle
were too uncomfortable, so he fitted it with inflated
rubber hoses. He patented the design in 1888.
There is no manufacturer's name;
they measure 2 inches (4.9 cm)
in diameter.*

NGK is a make of Japanese spark plug, while Eyquem, a French company, also makes spark plugs and automobile accessories. The spark-plug-shaped lighters date from 1990, whereas the Eyquem, resembling a slightly flattened tube of lipstick, dates from the 1930s.

The switch is on the bottom of the bottle. The flame pops out of the top. This comic 1950s model is an advertisement for Mercier Champagne. One of many of the unusual promotional gimmicks for the brand.

Heineken beer is Dutch. This
lighter was ordered in the
1980s by the brewer's
French office. It is a
"storm-proof" lighter,
covered in imitation
leather; the shape is
similar to the Zippo.

This make of German automobile is named after the daughter of their importer at the start of the twentieth century, Jellinek. Since then, Mercedes has come a long way and, like Ferrari on the facing page, they sell the license to their logo for promotional products. This Zippo dates from December 1990.

This is not an official souvenir lighter for the famous team created in 1929 by Enzo Ferrari, but a disposable butane model that was bought in a souvenir shop opposite the famous factory in Maranello, Italy.

This souvenir of Austria is made
by Piz and is a "striker lighter."
The rod is removed from
the gasoline reservoir by
unscrewing the cap, top left.
The ferrocerium strip is on
the right side of the lighter,
where the match is struck.
It dates from around 1935.

TOA means "Troupe d'Occupation en Allemagne," *and denotes the Allied forces that occupied Germany after the Second World War. The Rhine and the Danube are the symbols of the First French Army commanded by General de Lattre-Tassigny, which liberated France between Provence and the Rhine out to the river Danube to the east. The lighter was made in the 1950s, in the former East German Republic, by Weltünder.*

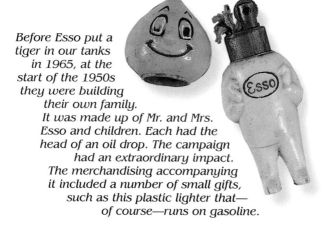

Before Esso put a tiger in our tanks in 1965, at the start of the 1950s they were building their own family. It was made up of Mr. and Mrs. Esso and children. Each had the head of an oil drop. The campaign had an extraordinary impact. The merchandising accompanying it included a number of small gifts, such as this plastic lighter that—of course—runs on gasoline.

Wynn's was a motor oil additive designed to improve engine performances. And it worked. The name of the model here is the Automatic Brother Lite lighter. It was made in Japan.

Heineken had the idea of ordering miniature beer mugs from the famous Delft porcelain factory that could be used as lighters. Other brewers followed suit. Such models can become the focus for a whole collection.

Reddy Kilowatt is a character much sought after by Zippo collectors. The electrical equipment company of the same name in Bradford, England was one of Zippo's first clients back at the start. The model featuring this logo was reissued in March 1998. It came in a presentation case containing the lighter on the left and a tape measure.

The Zippo "Slim," the slenderest of the Zippo models, here with the Coca-Cola logo. On the back is the address of one of their distributors: Paul St.-Onge Inc, St. Hyacinthe, Quebec. The bottle motif is in relief.

*Zippo fanatics like to collect series of lighters.
One such collector found a table and a pocket model,
at several years' interval, both
featuring the logo of the Illinois
Sports News. It is worth noting
that, since its creation in 1932,
Zippo has sold nearly
300 million lighters.*

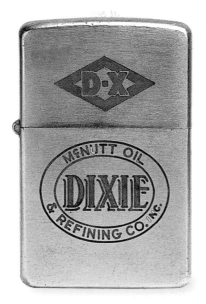

The Dixie gasoline refining company ordered these promotional lighters from Zippo in 1955. Note that, at the time, the colors were introduced into the hollows of the engraving, whereas today, silkscreen prints are mainly used.

Zippo and Coca Cola elected to reproduce old promotional models from between 1936 and 1940 for this July 1990 reissue. Note the characteristic stripes in the corner. The base is flat and bears the old patent number, 2032695.

Throughout its existence, the Zippo brand has also promoted itself by producing lighters displaying its own logo. This one dates from December 1987.

More than words could
ever say! This lighter
from June 1988 features
Zippo's different logos
since its creation in
1932. The company's
trading policy has
always been to offer
a lifetime guarantee
on its products,
summed up in the
slogan: "Works or
we fix it free."

This is how collectors like their lighters in general and Zippos in particular—new and in their box! Here is a "Slim" model with an insurance company logo.

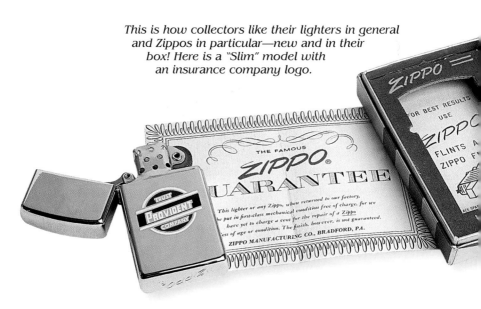

A Zippo made to promote Black & White Scotch Whisky could only be black and white. A regular model is used here, carrying the standard French health warning about alcohol. It helps to remember that cigarette smoking is not marvelous for the health either.

Index,
Acknowledgments,
and Bibliography

Index

The index features the main brands and models that appear in the book.

INDEX

INDEX

Acknowledgments

I would like to thank those collectors
who entrusted me with their treasures.
I am deeply grateful to:
Philippe Berry
Bernard Jean
Mathieu de Nanteuil
Daniel Lerasle

A C K N O W L E D G M E N T S

*I am no less grateful to Alain Berthon, who is a master
of the art of making fire by all means conceivable and feasible.
He has a boutique in the Marché Serpette of the Saint–Ouen "Flea-market,"
called "Stand très à l'étroit," Stand 13, allée 3, 110 rue des Rosiers,
94300 Saint-Ouen, France. Tel: + 33 1 40 12 10 58.
Tel. and fax: + 33 1 45 66 98 02.
Cell phone: + 33 6 82 67 76 75.*

*Another Parisian store, belonging to Romain Réa,
deals in old watches but also has a number of beautiful lighters on offer.
8 rue du Bac, 75007 Paris, Tel: + 33 1 42 61 43 44.
Fax: + 33 1 42 61 21 94.
Cell phone: + 33 6 09 17 32 76.
Web site: www.explorheure.com
He also has a stall at the Marché Dauphine
(1st floor, stand 233) of the Saint-Ouen "Flea-market":
138, rue des Rosiers, 94300 Saint–Ouen.*

*My gratitude as well to the Le Secq des Tournelles museum, rue Jacques Villon,
76000 Rouen. Tel: + 33 2 35 71 28 40. Fax: + 33 2 35 15 43 23,
from where the lighters on pages 20 (inventory number LS [1995] 372)
and 21 (inventory number LS [1995] 399) originate.
The museum has an amazing array of ironwork objects.*

Gratitude as well to Antoine Pascal, a brilliant, skillful photographer.

Bibliography

Faveton, Pierre. Autour du tabac, *Paris: Editions Massin, 1988.*

Kesaharu. Zippo, collection manual #1, #2, #3, #4, *Tokyo: World Photo Press, 1992–1996.*

Kroeber, Theodora. Ishi in Two Worlds, *Berkeley: University of California Press, 1988.*

La Fleur du mal, *Paris: Editions ACE, 1994.*

Poore, David. Zippo, the Great American Lighter, *Westchester, Pennsylvania: Schiffer Publishing, 1997.*

Wavrin, Patrice. Artisinat de tranchée et briquets de poilus (Craftwork of the Trenches and Poilu Lighters), *Louviers, France: Editions Ysec, 2001.*

Yates, Sarah. Smoking Accessories: A Collector's Guide, *London, UK: Miller's, 2000.*

In the same series

Collectible
POCKET KNIVES

Dominique Pascal

Flammarion

Collectible
CORKSCREWS

Frédérique Crestin-Billet

Collectible
WRISTWATCHES

René Pannier

Flammarion

Collectible
SNOWDOMES
Lélie Carnot

Flammarion

Collectible
MINIATURE CARS
Dominique Pascal

Flammarion

Collectible
PIPES
Jean Rebeyrolles

Flammarion

Collectible
MINIATURE
PERFUME BOTTLES

Anne Breton

Flammarion

Collectible
FOUNTAIN
PENS

Juan Manuel Clark

Flammarion

Collectible
PLAYING CARDS

Frédérique Crestin-Billet

Flammarion

Photographic Credits

*FA 1133-02-XII
Dépôt légal: 12/2002*